Mechanics Department in Physics Lessons and Problem Solving Methodology

Begmuradov Shohzod

© Taemeer Publications LLC
Mechanics Department in Physics Lessons and Problem Solving Methodology
by: Begmuradov Shohzod
Edition: September '2023
Publisher:
Taemeer Publications LLC (Michigan, USA / Hyderabad, India)

ISBN 978-93-5872-908-5

© **Taemeer Publications**

Book	:	Mechanics Department in Physics Lessons and Problem Solving Methodology
Author	:	Begmuradov Shohzod
Publisher	:	Taemeer Publications
Year	:	'2023
Pages	:	136
Title Design	:	*Taemeer Web Design*

In the Name of Abdulla Kadiri
Jizzakh State Pedagogical University
Faculty of Physics and Technological
Education Department
of Physics and Astronomy

CHAPTER 1
KINEMATICS

According to the purpose of studying the situation, properties and actions of existing bodies in nature and describing the processes associated with them, various simplified models are used in physics, that is, existing objects are replaced by their idealized copy - a model. For this purpose, mechanical simulations or models called material point, absolute (absolute) solid body, continuous (holistic) environment are used in the mechanics department of physics.

Any body whose geometric dimensions and shape are not taken into account and whose mass is concentrated at one point in the studied conditions is called a material point. The concept of a material point is a scientific abstraction. When we introduce this concept, we focus on the aspects that determine the main essence of the phenomenon under study, and do not take into account other features (geometric dimensions of the body, composition, internal state and changes in this state). In the science of physics, not only one body is studied, but also several sets of bodies are studied. These bodies can be considered as a set (system) of material points. One macroscopic body can be divided into small pieces, and these pieces can be imagined as a system (system) of interacting material points.

Each body itself can be a material point under one condition and not be a material point under another condition. The question of considering a body as a material point depends on the nature of the phenomenon under investigation. For example, when we consider the annual movement of the Earth around the Sun along its orbit, the Earth can be considered a material point, because the diameter of the Earth is so small that it cannot be considered in relation to the diameter of its orbit. According to the same considerations, when we observe the movement of the Moon in its orbit around the Earth, the ready movement from one city to another, and finally, the movement of a stone thrown (horizontally) from the top of a tower along the horizontal plane (or thrown vertically), they can be examples of the material point model. Therefore, if the size of the body is so small that it is not taken into account in relation to the scales of movement, such a body is considered a material point.

An absolutely rigid body is a body whose distance between two arbitrary points does not change during its motion. There is no absolute solid body in nature. It is known that any solid body is deformed under the influence of an external force, that is, its geometric dimensions and shape change to some extent. But depending on the nature of the problem, in most cases, the changes due to deformation can be ignored. An absolute solid is imagined to consist of a system of rigidly connected material points, like any macroscopic body.

The concept of a continuous medium is used to study the movement and equilibrium of liquids, gases, and deformable bodies. It is known that any material body is composed of atoms and molecules and has a discrete structure. But in order to simplify the matter, considering the matter as a continuous whole (integral) environment, the fact that it is composed of atoms and molecules is not taken into account.

In studying the laws of motion of bodies, it is important to clearly visualize the concepts of space and time. It is known that since all material bodies have volume, they occupy a certain place and are located in some way relative to each other. A body changes its position (position) due to its motion. This change naturally occurs in space and takes place over a period of time. Any mechanical process takes place in space at some point in time. Time is a physical quantity that expresses the sequence of events. The movement of bodies cannot be imagined in isolation from space and time. Therefore, it is considered that the existence of bodies and their movements occur in space and time. Space and time are crucial, historically evolving concepts in creating the physical landscape of the Universe. Newton's teaching on this is as follows: there is absolute (absolute) space and absolute time, which does not depend on any process; space is an eternally existing, boundless (infinitely large), immovable space, in which matter exists in various forms; space is homogeneous and its properties are the same in all directions; the properties of this space do not depend on the distribution and movement of substances in it and do not change over time. The distribution of matter and their movement in such a constant space is determined by the universal gravitation cone. According to Newton's point of view, time is absolute and passes uniformly, independent of the external environment and the movement of the body. Newton's theory of space and time is practically correct for mechanical motions observed under normal conditions (bodies, means of transportation, satellites, spaceships, planetary movements); this doctrine is based on the geometry of the Greek scientist Euclid. In Euclidean geometry, the sum of the interior angles of a triangle is 180°, and the shortest distance between two points is a straight line. It is not difficult to measure the sum of the interior angles of a triangle drawn on a small scale (scales, for example, the size of a sheet of paper). To what extent Euclidean geometry is correct on a much larger scale, or with what precision it can be used in practice, experience will certainly give us the answer.

At the beginning of the 20th century A. Einstein created the general theory of relativity. From this theory it follows that the real space of the Universe is a non-Euclidean space. According to this theory, the geometrical properties of space and the rate of passage of time depend on the distribution of matter in space and its movement. That is, the movement of space and matter are inextricably linked. Therefore, the general theory of relativity is also called the space-time theory. The distribution and movement of matter in space changes the interrelated geometry of space-time, and changes in the geometry of space-time determine the distribution and movement of matter in it. General relativity does not lead to the conclusion that Newton's theory of space and time is wrong. Experience shows that Newton's theory is true only in small areas of space taken on astronomical scales, and for short time intervals compared to those scales. On large scales—events involving metagalactic distances, as well as strong gravitational fields, deviations from Newton's laws occur. It should be said that if there are strong gravitational fields in some small areas of the Universe, the curvature of space and the change in the speed of time will be significantly manifested in these areas.

In the special theory of relativity created by A. Einstein in 1905, just like in Newtonian mechanics, time is considered homogeneous, and space is homogeneous and isotropic (the properties are the same in all directions). In this theory, it was proved that space and time cannot be considered separately, that time and space are related to each other, and that the space-time descriptions of bodies depend on their speeds determined in relation to a specific number system. According to this theory, time intervals and cross-sectional lengths are relative, depending on what reference systems they are measured in, that is, the length of a body (section) at rest relative to a reference system differs from the length of a moving reference system.

1.1. The position of the body in space.

Determining the position of an object in space means determining its position in space relative to other objects. An arbitrary body that allows determining the position of the studied body in space is called a reference body. In general, an arbitrary body - a car, the Earth, the Sun, stars can be considered as a counting body. Countable body alone is not enough to determine the position of bodies in space. If a reference object is selected, a coordinate axis passing through a point of the

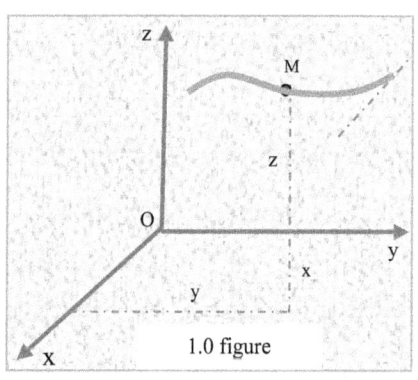

1.0 figure

reference object is drawn to determine the position of the studied object. The coordinate head is connected to the reference body. Then the position of an arbitrary point of the body in space is determined by its coordinates. In general, the coordinate (position) of an arbitrary material point M located on a straight line is expressed in the form M(x). If the value of x is negative, it means that the material point is located opposite the direction of the Ax axis from the count head (0), if it is positive, it is located in the direction of the Ax axis. The reference point and coordinate axes connected to it are called coordinate system. Coordinate system can be one-dimensional, two-dimensional, three-dimensional. A one-dimensional coordinate system allows determining the position of an arbitrary body in a straight line. If a material point is located in a plane, one coordinate axis alone will not be enough to determine its position. For this purpose, the second - Ou axis passing through the beginning of the counter and directed perpendicularly to the Ox axis is transferred and a two-dimensional coordinate system is introduced.

In general, the situation of a material point in the plane is determined by two numerical values corresponding to the axes OX and OU, and it is defined by the expression M (x; u). In life, sometimes it is necessary to determine the situation of objects located in space. For example, an electric lamp hanging from the ceiling of a room, a toy at the end of a tree in the middle of a room, or a book on a desk are neither in a straight line nor in a plane relative to a corner of the room (counting head). One more coordinate axis is introduced to determine the position of such bodies located in space. As a result, a three-dimensional coordinate system is created. In the three-dimensional coordinate system, the position of a material point is determined by three numerical values and is written in the form of M (x;u;z).

Algebra of vectors

One of them is defined by its numerical value and is called a scalar quantity or scalar quantity. Such quantities include surface area, volume, density, mass, amount of heat, amount of energy, etc. In order to fully express the second type of quantities, their directions should be given in addition to their numerical values. Such quantities are called vector quantities or vectors. Displacement, acceleration, force, torque are vector quantities.

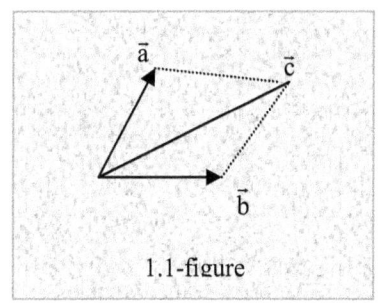

1.1-figure

Representation of vectors. If the end point is indicated by an arrow in the drawing, an arrow is placed over the letter that the vector is marked with in the text ($\vec{r}$). The numerical value of a vector is called its modulus or length, and r or $|\vec{r}|$ will be displayed. Vectors with equal length $\vec{r}_0$ and same direction are called mutually equal vectors. A vector whose length is equal to one unit is called a unit vector and is defined as: $\vec{r} = r \cdot \vec{r}_0$.

Vectors whose starting point can lie at any point in the plane or space are called free vectors. We work with free vectors, that is, we move vectors to the desired point. This makes it easier to perform actions on them. in turn, the homogeneity of space and time, that is, the equal strength of all their values, fully allows this.

Adding vectors. A vector whose sides are equal to the diagonal of a parallelogram consisting of these vectors is called the sum of two and vectors (Fig. 1.2):

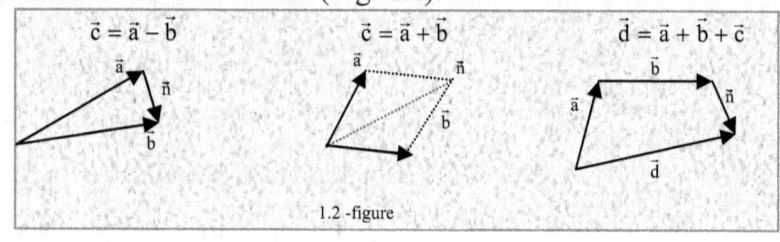

1.2 -figure

In this case, the vectors $\vec{a}$ and $\vec{b}$ are moved to point 0 and a parallelogram is formed using the vectors $\vec{a}$ ъ and $\vec{b}$ ъ which are parallel to them.

As can be seen from the figure 1.2, to add the vectors $\vec{a}$ and b, it is enough to move the beginning of the vector $\vec{b}$ to the end point of the vector $\vec{a}$ and connect the starting point of the vector $\vec{a}$ with the end point of the vector b. This is exactly what happens when several vectors are added (Figure 1.2).

$$\vec{d} = \vec{a} + \vec{b} + \vec{c}$$

Algebraic sum means adding the numerical values of quantities, and geometric sum means adding taking into account directions in addition to numerical values.

Subtraction of vectors. Subtracting $\vec{a}$ vector from $\vec{b}$ vector is done like adding $\vec{a}$ vector to $(-\vec{b})$ vector:

$$\vec{c} = \vec{a} - \vec{b} = \vec{a} + (-\vec{b})$$

Multiplication and division of vectors by numbers. Multiplying a vector by a number m means changing its modulus m times

$$\vec{c} = m\vec{a} = ma\vec{a}_0 = (ma)\vec{a}_0$$

Dividing a vector by n is done like multiplying it by 1/n, i.e

$$\vec{d} = \frac{\vec{a}}{n} = \frac{1}{n}\vec{a}$$

Scalar product of two vectors. The scalar product of two vectors is a scalar quantity equal to the product of the lengths of these vectors and the cosine of the angle between them (Fig. 1.3)

$$(\vec{a} \cdot \vec{b}) = a \cdot b \cdot \cos\alpha .$$

If $\alpha = \dfrac{\pi}{2}$, $\cos\alpha = 0$ and $(\vec{a}\cdot\vec{b}) = a\cdot b\cdot\cos\dfrac{\pi}{2} = 0$ will be. Therefore, the scalar product of mutually perpendicular vectors is equal to 0.

Vector product of two vectors. The vector product of two vectors $\vec{a}$ and $\vec{b}$ is called vector c such that it is perpendicular to the vectors $\vec{a}$ and $\vec{b}$ and the magnitude is equal to the face of the parallelogram made up of the sides and vectors, and the direction should be such that if the vector coincides with the forward movement of the drill, the movement of the drill bit corresponds with the transition from vector to vector comes, $\vec{c} = \left[\vec{a}\cdot\vec{b}\right]$ (Fig. 1.4). $\vec{c}$ the modulus of the vector c = a ×b ×sin f

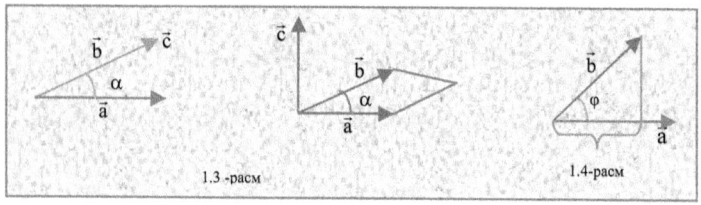

1.3 -расм   1.4-расм

1.2. Trajectory and path. An object passes through different points of space during motion. When these points are connected together, a line of some kind is formed. This line indicates the trajectory of the object. A trajectory is a line representing the trace left by a material point in space during its movement. For example, a falling meteorite in the night sky leaves a visible trajectory - a light trail (Fig. 1.5).

The trajectory of the billiard cue consists of broken lines. Many times you have seen a white trail behind an airplane flying very high on clear days. This trace is the plane's trajectory. The movement trajectory of objects consists of a line of arbitrary form. The trajectory of an object can be known before it starts moving. For example, the trajectory of trains, trams, trolleybuses is known in advance. In physics, it is important to calculate the movement trajectory of objects in advance.

For example, scientists predict the trajectories of spacecraft and satellites launched into space using other information about the movement. An object travels a certain distance while moving along a trajectory. The distance traveled by a material point along the trajectory for a certain time is called a path. A path can be measured, so it is a physical quantity. The road is marked with the letter L and S, and it is measured in units of length. In most cases, the trajectory of the object will not matter much. It is enough to know the initial and final position of the body to create a complete picture of the movement.

1.3. The speed of the object. In mechanics, a vector physical quantity called velocity is introduced to characterize the direction and speed of a point's movement. The velocity of a point at the moment of time t is a vector quantity equal to the first-order derivative obtained from the radius-vector of this point $\vec{v}$ with respect to time.

$$\vec{v} = \lim_{\Delta t \to 0} \frac{\Delta \vec{r}}{\Delta t} = \frac{d\vec{r}}{dt}.$$

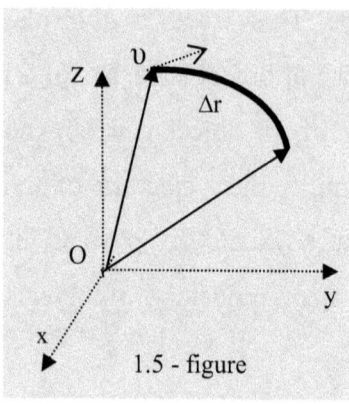

1.5 - figure

A motion whose trajectory is in a straight line and the amount of its velocity remains constant is called a rectilinear plane motion. During such motion, the material point traverses equal cross-sections at arbitrary but equal intervals of time. Naturally, rectilinear motion coincides with the displacement of the material point as shown in the figure, and they are also equal in quantity.

Therefore, displacement Δr can be replaced by the path ΔS it takes. Hence the expression for speed

$$\vec{\vartheta} = \lim_{\Delta t \to 0} \frac{\Delta \vec{r}}{\Delta t} = \lim_{\Delta t \to 0} \frac{\Delta S}{\Delta t} = \frac{dS}{dt}$$

(1.6)

is determined by Since the motion is flat

$$\vartheta = \frac{S}{t} \qquad (1.7)$$

can also be written as So, in a straight line, the speed is equal to the ratio of the traveled distance to the time taken to travel this route. In other words, speed is a quantity measured by the length of the path covered in a unit of time.

A road in a straight line. Knowing the speed of a material point in a straight line, it is possible to calculate the path traveled by it in a certain time. Let's find the vector expression of displacement using the expression (1.1).

$$\Delta \vec{s} = \vec{s} - \vec{s}_0 = \vec{v} \cdot (t - t_0).$$

The formula for calculating the path for the length of the displacement vector in a straight line is equal to the traveled path

$$\Delta s = s - s_0 = v \cdot (t - t_0)$$

And the path traveled by the body at arbitrary time t

$$s = s_0 + v \cdot (t - t_0)$$

is calculated using the formula. You can choose to start counting $t_0 = 0$ when learning to move. Then the displacement formula

$$\vec{s} = \vec{s}_0 + \vec{v} \cdot t$$

appears. The last formula is called the equation of motion of a material point.

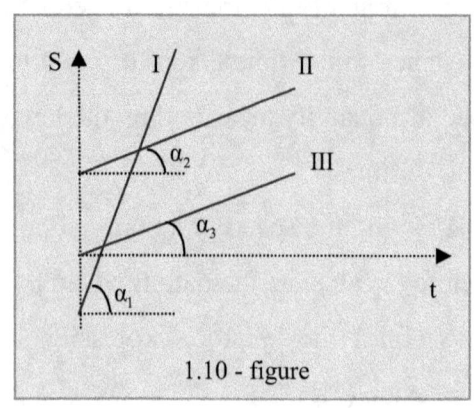

1.10 - figure

Calculating speed using a road graph. Using the graph in Figure 1.10, it is required to find the speed. For this, the value of s corresponding to arbitrary t is determined, that is, it is transferred from point A perpendicular to axes Os and Ot. Using the resulting right triangle, the tangent of angle a is determined

$$tg\alpha = \frac{AB}{s_0 B} = \frac{s-s_0}{t} = \upsilon.$$

Therefore, the tangent of the angle formed by the path graph with the time axis in a straight line movement represents the speed of this movement, i.e.

$$tg\alpha = \upsilon = \frac{s-s_0}{t} \qquad (1.8)$$

It is known from trigonometry that the greater the angle in the interval $0 \leq \alpha \leq 90^0$, the greater the tangent of this angle. It is possible to compare the graphs of the path for several objects and compare their velocities. Using the graph in Fig.

$$\alpha_1 > \alpha_2 > \alpha_3$$

i.e $\upsilon_1 > \upsilon_2 > \upsilon_3$ it follows that the speed of the first body is the greatest. Therefore, if the line representing the movement of the body on the path graph is directed at a large angle, the speed of this body will be the greatest. Expressing the time dependence of the path with the help of formulas, tables and graphs is important in the study of all movements found in nature.

Speed in straight line motion. The movement of bodies differs from each other by the speed of movement. For example, a car moving straight down the road will overtake a person moving straight down the road, and an airplane will overtake a car. In this case, it is said that the car is moving faster than the person, and the plane is moving faster than the car, i.e. faster.

The movement of these bodies differs from each other in their speed: the speed of a material point in a straight line is a physical quantity that expresses the ratio of the path traveled by the material point to the time it takes to travel this path.

Suppose that t_0 body moves during time to and during time to $\vec{s}_0$. Then the displacement of the body in time is $\vec{s}_0$, by definition, $\Delta t = t-t_0$ the vector $\Delta \vec{s} = \vec{s}-\vec{s}_0$ expression of the velocity formula

$$\vec{\upsilon} = \frac{\Delta \vec{s}}{\Delta t} = \frac{\vec{s}-\vec{s}_0}{t-t_0} \qquad (1.9)$$

while the scalar expression

$$\upsilon = \frac{\Delta s}{\Delta t} = \frac{s-s_0}{t-t_0} \qquad (1.10)$$

will have an appearance. The unit of speed is derived using the expression (1.7).

$$[v]=\frac{[s]}{[t]}=\frac{1m}{1s}=1\frac{m}{s}, \qquad [v]=1\frac{m}{s}.$$

The unit of speed is the speed of such an object in uniform motion, which travels a distance of 1 m per second.

1.4. Acceleration of the body. If we carefully observe the mechanical movement, we can notice that the same body moves at different speeds at different moments of time. For example; a car starting from a stationary position gradually increases its speed up to a certain value. When approaching a stop, it starts to reduce its speed. The concept of acceleration is introduced to characterize the change of speed as a function of time. Acceleration is denoted by the letter a. Let us assume that the speed of a moving body $\Delta\vec{\vartheta}=\vec{\vartheta}_2-\vec{\vartheta}_1$ at time t1 is v1, the speed at time t2. Let it change to the value of the velocity vector during the observation time interval $\Delta t = t_2 - t_1$. In that case, acceleration

$$a = \lim_{\Delta t \to 0} \frac{\Delta \vartheta}{\Delta t} = \frac{d\vartheta}{dt} \qquad (1.16)$$

is said to the expression. Therefore, the acceleration vector is equal to the first derivative of the velocity vector with respect to time. The acceleration value obtained in a very short time interval is also called its instantaneous value. In the international system of units, acceleration is measured in m/s2. It should be noted that the expression (1.16) evaluates the change of speed in terms of quantity and direction. Acceleration in motion, where the motion trajectory consists of a straight line, shows only the numerical value of the velocity changes over time. Only in curvilinear movement, the value of the speed can change both quantitatively and in terms of direction. Therefore, let's see how the above-mentioned kinematic quantities such as velocity and acceleration are in straight-line and curved movements. If the amount of speed increases by an equal value in equal time intervals, it is called uniformly accelerating ($\alpha>0$), and if it decreases to an equal value, it is called uniformly decelerating ($\alpha<0$). If the speed of a material point increases uniformly from the initial speed y0 to the final speed y in the time interval t, the acceleration is positive (a>0),

$$a = \frac{\vartheta - \vartheta_0}{t}$$

will be equal to From this formula, the final velocity is found as follows

$$\vartheta = \vartheta_0 + at.$$

If the motion is uniformly decelerating, the final velocity y will be smaller than the initial velocity (υ_0). Acceleration then

$$a = \frac{\vartheta_0 - \vartheta}{t}$$

will be negative (a<0). In straight-line, uniformly accelerated motion, the direction of the acceleration vector coincides with the direction of the velocity vector. Their directions are opposite in a smooth decelerating motion. In this case, the final velocity

$$\vartheta = \vartheta_0 - at$$

is found by expression. If the body stops in a linear decelerated motion $\upsilon = 0$, or

$$\vartheta = at$$

the initial velocity is found by

1.5. Displacement, velocity and acceleration in curvilinear motion.

It is known that if an object moving in a straight line is subjected to a force opposite to the direction of motion, the

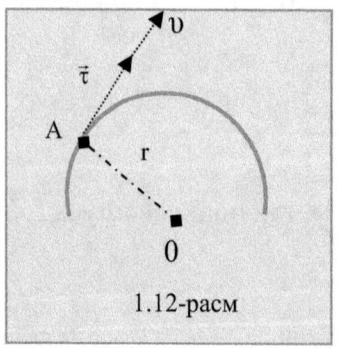

1.12-расм

amount of velocity of the object will decrease, but the direction will not change. Now let's consider the case where the force acts on the body at an angle to the direction of its velocity. If a string is attached to an object moving in a straight line and we pull it sideways, we make it move in a curved line, where the force must act at an angle to the velocity of the object. Therefore, the object moves in a curved line under the influence of the force whose direction is at an angle to the velocity of the object. Depending on the magnitude and direction of the force acting on the body, curved movements can be different. Motions along a circle, parabola, ellipse, etc. are the simplest types of curvilinear motion.

Experiments show that when the force acting on a curved object from the side stops, it begins to move in a straight line without trying to follow the trajectory of movement.

Since this conclusion is also valid for a body moving in a curved line, we conclude that the speed of a body moving in a circle at any point is directed by the effort applied to this point of the circle. Circular motion is the simplest case of curvilinear motion. Let's look at this action. Let us assume that a material point moves uniformly along a circle of radius r.

Δt during the interval the material traverses the arc of the point ΔS, and at this point it turns the corner $\Delta \varphi$.

$$\Delta S = \Delta \varphi r.$$

Divide both sides of the equation by Δt.

$$\frac{\Delta S}{\Delta t} = r \frac{\Delta \varphi}{\Delta t}.$$

In this

$$\omega = \lim_{\Delta \to 0} \frac{\Delta \varphi}{\Delta t} = \frac{d\varphi}{dt}. \qquad (1.17)$$

Expression (1.17) is called angular velocity. So, the angular velocity shows how much the angle of rotation changes in a unit of time

$$\omega = \lim_{\Delta t \to 0} \frac{\Delta \omega}{\Delta t} = \frac{d\omega}{dt}.$$

(1.18)

(1.18) quantity is called the linear acceleration of a material point moving along a circle. Therefore, linear velocity and angular velocity are related as follows

$$\upsilon = \omega r.$$

The time taken for one full rotation of a material point is called the rotation period (T). Since a material point moving along a circle in one period is turned by 2π radian angle, the angular velocity is equal to

$$\omega = \frac{2\pi}{T}.$$

From this, it follows that the unit of measurement of angular velocity in the XV system is the radian. 1 radian=570 is equal to 3 or 3600= radians. The number of revolutions per unit time is called frequency. Frequency is the inverse of period

$$\nu = \frac{1}{T}.$$

If we express the angular velocity in terms of frequency

$$\omega = 2\pi\nu \qquad (1.19)$$

Expression (1.19) is also called circular frequency. If the

frequency of rotation of a material point is known, its linear speed can be found, i.e

$$\upsilon = 2\pi\nu r. \quad (1.20)$$

If the object is moving uniformly along a circle, the modulus of the linear velocity υ =const will be constant. It does not follow that a material point moving uniformly along a circle is in motion without acceleration. In this movement, the direction of the linear velocity of the material point changes continuously. At each point of the trajectory, the instantaneous velocity of the material point is tentatively directed to that point. To find the instantaneous acceleration, we take the limit from the expression (1.20).

$$a = \frac{\upsilon}{r} \lim_{\Delta t \to 0} \frac{\Delta \upsilon}{\Delta t}. \quad (1.21)$$

When the observation time approaches Δt zero, $(\Delta t \to 0)$ the length of the arc begins to approach the length of the arc Δl, and ΔS point B begins to approach point A. Acceleration is directed along the radius towards the center of the circle. Therefore, this magnitude, which shows the change in direction of velocity, is called centripetal acceleration.

EXAMPLES OF PROBLEM SOLVING

Issue 1. A material point moving in one direction along a straight line moved with a speed of 4 m/s in the first half of the path, and with a speed of 8 m/s in the second half. Find the average speed on the total road covered.

Given: $v_1 = 4$ м/с, $v_2 = 8$ м/с.

Need to find: $<\vec{v}> = ?$

Solution: The average speed is determined by the ratio of the total distance s to the time t. That is $v = s/t$. Half of the path is covered by the material point at time $t = (s/2)/v = s/2v$, and the other half at time $t = (c/2v)$. In that case

$$t = t_1 + t_2 = \frac{s}{2v_1} + \frac{s}{2v_2} = \frac{s(v_1 - v_2)}{2v_1 v_2}.$$

originates. If we put the last expression of t in this formula into the average speed

$$<\vec{v}> = \frac{s}{t} = \frac{2v_1 v_2}{v_1 + v_2}.$$

originates. We count

$$<\vec{v}> = \frac{2v_1 v_2}{v_1 + v_2} = \frac{2 \cdot 8 \cdot 4}{4 + 8} = \frac{64}{12} \approx 5{,}33 \frac{m}{c}.$$

Answer: $<\vec{v}> = 5{,}33 \frac{m}{c}$.

Issue 2. Body $x = \frac{6t - t^3}{8}$ moving along a straight line according to the law expressed by the formula. Find the average speed and acceleration of the body in the time interval from t1=2s to t2=6s.

Given: $x=\dfrac{6t-t^3}{8}$, $t_1=2$ c, $t_2=6$ c.

Need to find: $\langle \vec{\upsilon} \rangle =?$ $a=?$

Solution: Taking the first and second time derivatives from the equation of motion of the body $x=\dfrac{6t-t^3}{8}$, we find $\upsilon=\upsilon(t)$ and $a=a(t)$:

$$\vec{\upsilon}=\frac{dx}{dt}=6-\frac{3}{8}\cdot t^2, \qquad \vec{a}=\frac{d\upsilon}{dt}=\frac{d^2x}{dt^2}=-\frac{6}{8}\times t.$$

Given the values 0-6s for time, we calculate the corresponding numerical values of the speed and write them in the table below.

t, c	0	1	2	3	4	5	6
υ, м\c	6	5,625	4,5	2,625	0	- 3,375	- 7,5

Putting these values of time and speed on the coordinate axes on a certain scale, we draw a speed graph (Fig. 1)

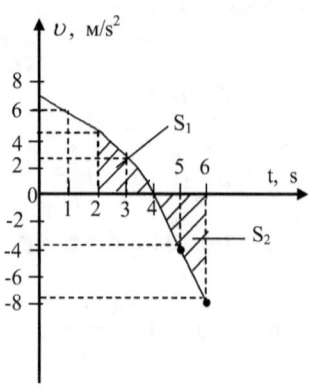

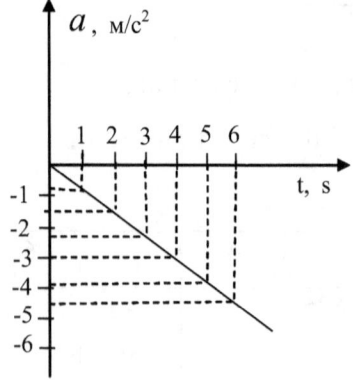

We calculate the accelerations in the time interval from 0 to 6 and write them in the table below.

t, c	0	1	2	3	4	5	6
a, м/с^2	0	- 0,75	- 1,5	- 2,125	- 3,0	- 3,75	- 4,5

Using the values from this table, we plot the

acceleration graph. (Figure 2). The average speed of the body: $<\overline{\upsilon}>=\dfrac{s_1+s_2}{t_1-t_2}$.

Here, s1 and s2 are the dashed surfaces on the velocity graph, which are numerically equivalent to the distance traveled. To find this distance

$$ds = \upsilon\, dt$$

to expression $\upsilon = 6 - \dfrac{3}{8}t^2$, and integrate over the time interval from 2s to 4s and from 4s to 6s, since after 4s the direction of the velocity changes:

$$s = \int_2^4 (6-\tfrac{3}{8}t^2)dt + \int_4^6 -(6-\tfrac{3}{8}t^2)dt = \int_2^4 6\,dt - \tfrac{3}{8}\int_2^4 t^2 dt - \int_4^6 6\,dt + \tfrac{3}{8}\int_4^6 t^2 dt =$$

$$= 6(4-2) - \tfrac{3}{8}\left[\tfrac{t^3}{3}\right]_2^4 - 6(6-4) + \tfrac{3}{8}\left[\tfrac{t^3}{3}\right]_4^6 = 12\text{i}\ .$$

So, the average speed of the body is:

$$<\overline{\upsilon}> = \dfrac{12\,\text{M}}{(6-2)\text{c}} = 3\dfrac{\text{M}}{\text{c}}$$

Average acceleration of the body:

$$<a> = \dfrac{-4{,}5\tfrac{\text{M}}{\text{c}^2} + (-15)\tfrac{\text{M}}{\text{c}^2}}{2} = -3\dfrac{\text{M}}{\text{c}^2}.$$

Answer: $<\overline{\upsilon}>=3\dfrac{\text{M}}{\text{c}}$; $<a>=-3\dfrac{\text{M}}{\text{c}^2}$;

Issue 3. What is the speed of an object falling freely to the ground in the sixth second?

Given: t=6 с, g=9,8 м/с².

Need to find: v=?

Solution: The free fall speed of an object is determined using the formula $v=gt$.

We calculate: $v=gt = 9{,}8$ м/с² · 6 с $= 38{,}8$ м/с.

Answer: the object falling to the ground reaches a speed of $v =38.8$ m/s in the seventh second.

Issue 4. Two objects are successively thrown from the same point and with the same initial speed v_0=34.5 m/s vertically upwards with an interval of τ=0.6 s. How much time and at what height will they meet each other after the first object is launched?

Given: v_0 =34,5 m/s, τ= 0,6 с, g=9,8 m/s².

Need to find: t=? h=?

Solution: We count the time from the moment the first object is thrown. Let the x-axis point vertically upwards. In that case, v_0 should be considered positive, and g should be considered negative. The height of the rise of the first body at time t

$$h=v_0 t - \frac{gt^2}{2}.$$

The height of the second object's ascent is expressed by a similar formula, but for the same instant of time since it was thrown later

$$h_2 = v_0(t-\tau) - \frac{g(t-\tau)^2}{2}.$$

The objects meet each other when the heights of the rise are equal. Therefore:

$$v_0 t - \frac{gt^2}{2} = v_0 t - v_0 \tau - \frac{gt^2}{2} - \frac{g\tau^2}{2} + gt\tau,$$

and from this bodies with each other

$$t = \frac{v_0}{g} + \frac{\tau}{2}$$

will meet later.

We calculate: t=(34,5/9)+(0,6/2)=3,82 c. Height of objects meeting each other:

$$h = v_0 \left(\frac{v_0}{g} + \frac{\tau}{2} \right) - \frac{g\left(\frac{v_0}{g} + \frac{\tau}{2} \right)^2}{2} = \frac{v_0^2}{2g} - \frac{g\tau^2}{2}$$

$$h = \frac{(34,5)^2}{2 \cdot 9,8} - \frac{9,8 \cdot (0,6)^2}{g} = 60,286 \text{ м}.$$

Solution: t=3,82 c, h=60,286 m.

Issue 5. A flywheel rotating at an angular speed of 300 rpm t=0.6 min. brakes inside. Assuming the motion of the flywheel to be in uniform deceleration, find how many revolutions it takes before it comes to a complete stop.

Given: v =300 rou/min= 5 айл/с, t=0,6 min=36 с.

Need to find: N=?

Solution: Since the final velocity is zero, the angular displacement during the time elapsed before the flywheel comes to a complete stop can be found from the following equation:

$$\varphi = \frac{\varepsilon t^2}{2},$$

here $\varepsilon = \frac{\omega}{t}$. Now we find here

$$\varphi = \frac{\omega t}{2},$$

$$\omega = 2\pi v = 2\pi \cdot 5 \frac{rad}{c} = 10\pi \frac{rad}{c}.$$

Until Mohovik stops:

$$N = \frac{\varphi}{2\pi} = \frac{\omega t}{4\pi} = \frac{10\pi \cdot 36}{4\pi} = 90 \text{ марта}$$

has become.

Answer: N=90 times.

Issue 6. The frequency of rotation of the disk of the surface grinding machine $v = 600 \frac{1}{\text{мин}}$. The period of disk rotation is T, the angular velocity ω. Find the linear velocity v of a point R=50 cm from the center of the disc.

Given: $\nu = 600\dfrac{1}{\text{мин}} = 10\dfrac{1}{\text{с}}$, R=50 см=0,5 м.

Need to find: v=?

Solution: The rotation period of the disc

$$T = \dfrac{1}{\nu} = \dfrac{1}{10\,\text{с}^{-1}} \approx 0{,}10\,\text{с}.$$

Angular velocity:

$$\omega = \dfrac{2\pi}{T} = 2\pi\nu = 2\cdot 3{,}14\cdot 10\,\dfrac{\text{rad}}{\text{с}} = 60{,}28\,\dfrac{\text{rad}}{\text{с}},$$

linear velocity:

$$\upsilon = \omega\cdot R = 60{,}28\,\dfrac{\text{rad}}{\text{с}}\cdot 0{,}5\,\text{м} = 30{,}14\,\dfrac{\text{м}}{\text{с}}.$$

Answer: υ=30,14 м/с.

Issues for independent solution
Kinematics of rectilinear motion

The car traveled the distance between two cities at a speed $v_1 = 60$ km/h. On the way back, its speed was $0.5\ v_1$. What is the average speed of the car during the entire flight?

A material point is moving in a straight line. At a distance of 1000 m from the starting point, it turns back and stops after traveling a distance of 1200 m in the opposite direction. What is the final displacement and the distance traveled.

A person moving with constant speed and direction is passing under a lantern hanging at a height h above the ground. If the height of the person is equal to h, find the speed of displacement of the edge of the shadow of his head relative to the ground.

Two cars are moving along highways intersecting at an angle with constant speeds u1 and u2. Find the speed and direction of one car relative to the other. How long after they meet at the intersection will the distance between the cars be equal to S?

The distance between two metro stations is 1.5 km. The first half of this distance was covered by the train with uniform acceleration (a1=0.13 m/s2), and the second half with uniform deceleration (a2=-0.13 m/s2)? What is the maximum speed of the train?

A body moves with uniform acceleration from rest and travels a distance of 7 m in the fourth second after the start of the movement. What distance does it travel in the first second?

1. At what speed should the plane fly from east to west on the equator so that the sun appears to the passengers to be still in the sky?

2. The rotation period of the Earth satellite is q min, its linear speed in its orbit is 7.8 km/s. At what height is the satellite's orbit above the earth's surface.

3. What is the linear speed of movement of points on the earth's surface at 540 latitude.

4. The wheel rotates with uniform acceleration and after 10 revolutions from the beginning of the motion, it has reached an angular velocity of 20 rad/s. What is the angular acceleration of the wheel?

The point is moving along a circle with a constant tangential acceleration of 0.1 m/s2, and the linear speed of the point's rotation has reached 79.2 cm/s by the end of the fifth revolution. What is the radius of a circle?

Find the angle between the radius of the wheel and the direction of full acceleration at the end of the first second of motion. The wheel radius is 10 cm. It is spinning with a constant angular acceleration of 3.14 rad/s2.

CHAPTER II
LAWS OF DYNAMICS

2.1. Newton's first law

Now we will consider the reasons for the movement of bodies, the laws of their interaction. Dynamics is a branch of mechanics that studies the causes of body motion. Dynamics is the study of the motion of a body and determines the forces that act on it when it moves. Newton's laws are the basis of dynamics. Until now, we have taken as a basis the speed and acceleration of the body's motion in the study of mechanical motion. But we have not answered the questions of why a body at rest moves, why a body moves in a straight line or a uniform variable motion, why a body moves in a circular motion, and what are the reasons for acceleration in these movements. The next task is to determine the connection between the movement of the body and the force. Aristotle, who lived in the 4th century BC, was the first to answer the question about the relationship between force and motion, saying that a force must act on a body to move in a horizontal plane. Aristotle explained that a body moves under the influence of a force because its state of rest is natural. Italian physicist Galileo Galilei, 2000 thousand years after Aristotle, said that just as the rest state of the body is

Isaak Newton
(1642-1727)

natural, so is its movement with constant speed in the horizontal plane. The teachings of these two great scientists do not contradict each other, because if there is no force acting on the body, it will eventually stop. Aristotle did not take into account the change in the rest state of bodies, while Galileo did. He says that the body will move forever with a constant speed only if it is free from these effects, taking into account the resistance of the air to the bodies, friction, the attraction of the bodies to the Earth and other effects. G. Galileo mentioned the idea that the main reason for bodies to stop moving is some kind of influence that opposes the movement and changes the movement, that is, the speed. The great English scientist Isaac Newton studied the works of scientists who lived before him, summarized them, and in 1667, in his book called "Mathematical Foundations of Natural Philosophy", he stated the three main laws of dynamics. Newton's first law: There are systems of reference in which the body remains at rest or moves in a straight line if no force acts on the body or if the forces acting on it are mutually compensated (if the acting force is zero). The first half of this definition, which is that the body is "at rest," is easy to understand. If there is no external influence on the body, it will not move. Why doesn't the second half of the definition say "rectilinear plane motion" or "plane motion"? Because we have seen in kinematics that there are two types of rectilinear movement - straight and variable, in variable movement the speed changes and acceleration is created. That's why it's called "smooth motion". The reason for the addition of the word "straight line" is that such motions are of two types - rectilinear motion and curvilinear motion. As we have seen in straight-line motion with a curve, normal acceleration is produced. This causes a change in motion. Therefore, the second half of Newton's first law is defined as "in uniform motion in a straight line." Body motion is expressed in number systems. But Newton's first law is correctly expressed only for the number systems under consideration. The resulting number system will be associated with an arbitrary number body. For example, with the Earth, with the Sun. Newton's first law is valid for this system if the body is in rectilinear plane motion relative to the resulting system. Newton's first law is called the law of inertia. The property of the observed object to maintain its state of rest or straight-line plane motion when it is affected by the objects in the environment surrounding it is called inertia. Therefore, Newton's first law is the law of inertia, and the frame of reference in which it is applied is called the inertial frame of reference. When the bus starts moving, the passengers inside the bus will move backwards. This is an example of inertia. In this case, the bus is a number system.

2.2. Force and mass. Newton's first law states that an observed body is not affected by another body, that is, bodies do not interact. If observed objects interact, the states or motions of the objects change. Therefore, the cause that changes the motion or rest state of bodies is called force. When a body's position or motion changes under the influence of a force, its speed changes, that is, acceleration is created.

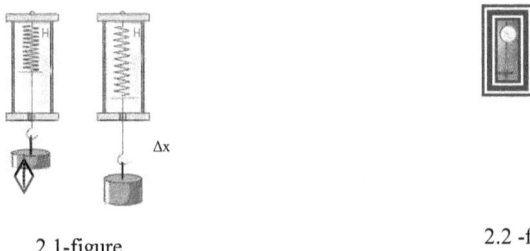

2.1-figure   2.2 -figure

For example, when a steam engine is connected to a stationary car, the car starts moving. When a steam locomotive starts moving from a station or approaches a station, its speed changes and acceleration is generated. This manifestation of power is called dynamic manifestation of power. But to consider force only as a cause that changes motion does not give its full meaning. For example, if we drop an object from above, it will move under the influence of the earth's gravity. Let's hang it with a net at a certain height without lowering it to the ground. The object stops moving, but the earth still continues to pull on it. But the body does not move. At this time, under the influence of the body, the shape of the mesh changes and some pressure force is applied to it. The gravity of the earth and the reaction force of the table when we put an elastic soft spring under the table under its influence, the spring is compressed without moving. So, interaction can move body parts relative to each other and change their shape or size. This manifestation of force is called static manifestation of force. Summarizing the cases seen above, we can define force as follows: the interaction that changes the movement or shape of bodies, or both at the same time, is called force. To measure force, we must first choose a unit of force. Then, by comparing the amount of force with this unit, the value of the force is determined. Using the static manifestation of force, it can be measured using spring dynamometers or spring scales. The extension Dx of the springs in these gauges should be proportional to the applied force (Fig. 2.1). Based on the above, we can derive the following definitions of force and ensure their equivalence. A force is a tool that moves a body. A force is a physical quantity that causes a change in the direction of movement of an object. A force is the cause of a change in the body's movement or shape. So, if a force acts on an object, its velocity also changes. However, it should be noted that the effect of force is not only manifested in the acceleration of the movement of objects, it is also possible to change the shape of objects (deformation) under the influence of force. The force is measured using a dynamometer (Fig. 2.2). The magnitude of the force giving acceleration of 1 m/s2 to a body with a mass of 1 kg in 1 second is 1 N. The quantity that describes the interaction of bodies in terms of quantity and direction is called force. So, force is a vector quantity. Let's get acquainted with the concept of mass, one of the main physical quantities. All objective material entities are a form of matter and have mass.

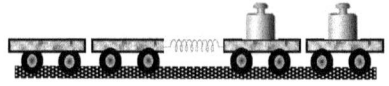

2.3 figure

For this, let's look at the following experiment. When we place a spring between the carts on a smooth bench (Figure 2.3), compress them tightly and release them, the same constant force is exerted by the compressed spring on both carts. Under the influence of this constant (unchanging) force, the acceleration of the loaded cart is less than the acceleration of the unloaded cart. Therefore, the acceleration of bodies under the influence of a certain force does not depend only on the applied force, but also on the physical property, which depends on the change in the amount of the substance that makes up the body. This is called inertia of the body. Therefore, the mass of an object is a measure of its inertia. Therefore, the mass in this state is called inert mass. In classical mechanics, the mass of a body is considered constant during motion when the speed of the body is much smaller than the speed of light. The mass of an object also represents the amount of matter contained in it. For example, if we turn water into ice under stable experimental conditions, its volume will not change. In the event of electrolysis, the substance released at the electrode also represents the quantity, these phenomena cannot be explained on the basis of inertness.

In our daily life, we measure body mass using weighing scales. The SI unit of mass is the kilogram (kg), which is equal to the mass of one cubic decimeter of pure water at a temperature of 4°C. The ability of a body to maintain a state of rest or motion is called inertia. The physical quantity describing the inertia of a body is called mass. Therefore, a body with a larger mass is more inert. Mass is a scalar quantity. The amount of matter in a body is also called mass. We can find the mass of any substance using the following formula.

$m = \rho \cdot V$

Here ρ is density of matter, V is volume. Mass is measured in kilograms (kg). The density of a substance depends on the temperature, that is, if the temperature increases, the density decreases. The geometrical position of a body in space is called volume. Volume is a scalar quantity. It is necessary to know that the volume of water at 4°C is the smallest and the density is the largest.

2.3. Newton's second law

Now let's define the relationship between force, mass and

acceleration. The relationship between these physical quantities is expressed by Newton's second law. Newton's second law can be defined as the force acting on a body is equal to the mass of the body multiplied by the acceleration of the body under the influence of this force. This is Newton's second law, and its mathematical expression is as follows

$$F = m\,a. \qquad (2.1)$$

Newton's second law is also called the law of motion. If instead of the acceleration in the formula (2.1) we put its expression through the speed $a = \dfrac{d\upsilon}{dt}$ and take into account that the mass is constant,

$$F = m\frac{d\upsilon}{dt} = \frac{d(m\upsilon)}{dt} \qquad (2.2)$$

the expression originates. This is a general expression of Newton's second law. The following conclusions follow from these:

1. *The force depends on whether the body is at rest or in motion. Because the speed changes under the influence of the force and creates acceleration.*

2. *When the force is constant, the body is in uniformly accelerated motion. Because the acceleration of the body does not change.*

3. *Experiments show that if a body is acted upon by several*

forces, it will have a certain acceleration in the direction of each force, as if it were not acted upon by other forces.

This is usually called the principle of independence of forces. But since the force is a vector quantity, the motion of the body, and the resultant force resulting from the vectorial (geometric) addition of the forces

$$R = F_1 + F_2 \qquad (2.3)$$

behavior under the influence is studied. As an example, let's look at the forces F1 and F2 acting on the object forming a mutual angle. We draw a parallelogram on these forces to determine the resultant force.

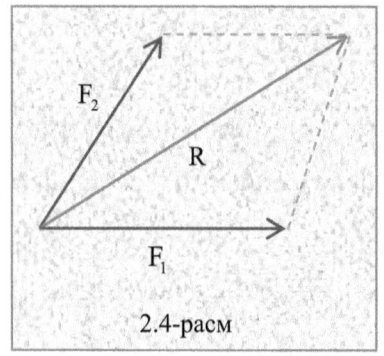

2.4-расм

The diagonal of the parallelogram represents the resultant force (Fig. 2.4). The body moves in the direction of this resultant force. Depending on the angle between the forces, the resultant force also changes, that is, with an increase in the angle, the magnitude of the sum decreases. Using Newton's second law, let's express the unit of force in the International System of Units (SI). If a body with a mass of 1 kg receives an acceleration of 1 m/s2 in the direction of force, this value of force is taken as a unit of force and is called Newton (N).

2.4. Newton's third law

All objects in nature interact. For example, if the bus driver suddenly drives him, we see that the passenger sitting on the seat inside him hits the backrest of the seat, and the backrest, in turn, affects the passenger. In this case, forces exist due to their interaction. Newton's third law is defined as follows. If the first body acts on the second body with a force F1, then the second body also acts on the first body with a force F2, these forces are equal in magnitude and opposite in direction along the straight line connecting them.

$$\vec{F_1} = -\vec{F_2}$$

(2.4)

Newton's third law is called the law of action or reaction.
If we apply Newton's second law to the above formula, it will look like this

$$m_1 \cdot a_1 = -m_2 \cdot a_2$$

from this

$$a_1 = -\frac{m_2}{m_1} \cdot a_2 \qquad (2.5)$$

Consequently, the interacting bodies move with an acceleration inversely proportional to their mass and opposite to each other.

In the example in Figure 2.5, there is a third-body compressed spring that gives acceleration to the carts. If we put the expression of accelerations in formula (2.2) through speeds, it takes the following form

$$m_1 \cdot \frac{dv_1}{dt} = -m_2 \cdot \frac{dv_2}{dt} \qquad (2.6)$$

Or since m1 and m2 are constants

$$d(m_1 \cdot v_1) + d(m_2 \cdot v_2) = 0 \qquad \text{or}$$

$$d(m_1 \cdot v_1 + m_2 \cdot v_2) = 0$$

Since the differential of the invariant quantity is equal to zero,

$$m_1 \cdot v_1 + m_2 \cdot v_2 = \text{const}$$

originates. Since the observed two bodies interact only and have no other influence on them, the momentum of the closed system consisting of these two bodies is equal to the vector sum of the momentums of the bodies and remains constant.

$$m_1 v_1 = m_2 v_2 \qquad (2.7)$$

This is called the law of conservation of momentum. This law can be generalized for a system of bodies. Reference systems that obey or obey Newton's laws are called inertial reference systems. Reference systems in which Newton's laws of dynamics are true are called inertial reference systems. Newton's laws of mechanics are not valid all the time, they are valid only in cases where the speed of the body is much smaller than the speed of light, taken in relation to inertial reference systems. When moving from one inertial frame of reference to another inertial frame of reference, the body's speed, body momentum, and kinetic energy do not change. Interaction refers to a change in the state of motion of bodies as a result of the impact of bodies.

EXAMPLES OF PROBLEM SOLVING

Issue 1. An unloaded car with a mass of 5 t moved with an acceleration of 0.5 m/s2. The loaded car starts moving under the influence of gravity as before and reaches a speed of 2 m/s after 6 seconds. Find the mass of the loaded load.

Given: $m_1 = 5T = 5 \cdot 10^3$ kg; $a_1 = 0,5$ м/с²; $t = 0,6$ с; $\upsilon = 2$ м/с.

Need to find: $m_2 = ?$

Solution: The drag force of the vehicle is determined by the expression based on Newton's second law $F = m_1 a_1$. The total mass of the loaded car $(m_1 + m_2)$ is affected by the force F as before

$$a = \frac{F}{m_1 + m_2} = \frac{m_1 a_1}{m_1 + m_2}$$

gets acceleration. The acceleration of a truck can be found using the formula for the velocity of a uniformly accelerated motion without initial velocity $\upsilon=at$:

$$a=\frac{\upsilon}{t}.$$

Let's equate both expressions of accelerations

$$\frac{m_1 a_1}{m_1+m_2}=\frac{\upsilon}{t},$$

and from this

$$m_2=\frac{m_1(a_1 t-\upsilon)}{v}$$

we come to the formula and calculate

$$m_2=\frac{5\cdot 10^3\left(0,5\frac{m}{c^2}\cdot 6c-2\frac{m}{c}\right)}{2\frac{m}{c}}=2,5\cdot 10^3\,\text{кг}.$$

Answer: The mass of the load $m_2=2,5\cdot 10^3\,\text{кг}$

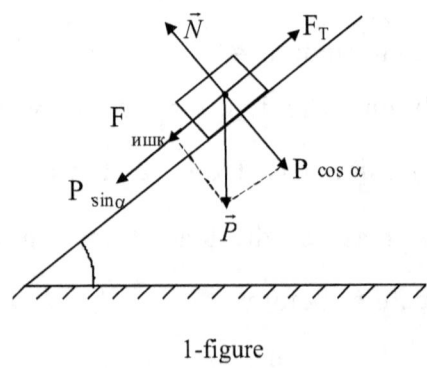

1-figure

Issue 2.

friction is 0.05. How far does the load move in 2 seconds?

Given: P=1000H, α=30⁰, F_T=800H,

μ=0,05, t=2 с.

Need to find: S=?

Solution: $\vec{P}$ we divide the power into two components. One of them is parallel to the inclined plane and its value is equal to P·sinα. The second is perpendicular to the inclined plane, its value is equal to P·cosα. The equation of motion of a load moving up an inclined plane is as follows:

$F_T - F_{is} - P \cdot \sin\alpha = ma$.

The friction coefficient formula to find the spark plug

$$\mu = \frac{F_{is}}{P\cos\alpha}$$

we use . As a result

$F_{is} = \mu \cdot P\cos\alpha$

an expression is generated.

$F_T - \mu P\cos\alpha - P\sin\alpha = ma = \dfrac{P}{g} \cdot a$.

we put the value of into the equation of motion:

$$a = \left(\frac{F_T}{P} - \mu\cos\alpha - \sin\alpha\right) \cdot g$$

we form the expression. Using the formula for distance traveled in uniformly accelerated motion,

$$S = \frac{at^2}{2} = \left(\frac{F_T}{P} - \mu\cos\alpha - \sin\alpha\right) \cdot \frac{gt^2}{2}$$

we come to the result.
We calculate:

$$S = \left(\frac{800N}{1000N} - 0{,}05\cos 30^0 - \sin 30^0\right) \cdot \frac{9{,}8\frac{m}{c}(2c)^2}{2} \approx 5\,\text{м}.$$

Answer: $S \approx 5\,\text{м}$

Issue 3. A model of a rocket with an initial mass m0=1.2 kg is rising vertically in the gravitational field of the earth. If the speed of the 0.4 kg gas stream that is ejected from the rocket every second is 800 m/s, what speed will the rocket reach relative to the ground 1 s after the start of the movement? The initial speed of the rocket $υ_0 = 0$.

Given: $υ'=800\,\text{м/с}$, $\dfrac{\Delta m}{\Delta t}=0{,}4\,\text{кг/с}$, $m_0=1{,}2\,\text{кг}$, $t=1\text{с}$.

Need to find: $υ =?$

Solution: To solve the problem, we use Newton's second law in the following form: $\vec{F}dt=d\vec{p}$;

where - $d\vec{p}_1$ is the change in the rocket momentum under the jet effect of the gas flow, which is equal to:

$$\vec{dp}_1 = \left(m_0 - \frac{\Delta m}{\Delta t}\cdot t\right)d\vec{υ}.$$

$\vec{dp}_2$ - the impulse of the ejected gas stream:

$$d\vec{p}_2 = \frac{\Delta m}{\Delta t} \cdot \vec{v}' dt$$

$\vec{F}$ - is the force of gravity, which at the initial time is equal to $\vec{F}=m_0\vec{g}$. $\vec{F}$, $d\vec{P}_1$, $d\vec{P}_2$ - we put the expressions of s into equation (1):

Taking into account that the speed of the gas flow coming out of the rocket $\vec{v}'$ is directed in the same direction as the acceleration of free fall, and that speed is directed in the opposite direction $\vec{v}$, we make the last equation into the following scalar form:

$$(m_0 - \frac{\Delta m}{\Delta t} \cdot t)d\vec{v} = -(m_0\vec{g} - \frac{\Delta m}{\Delta t}\vec{v}')dt.$$

Both sides of this equation

$$(m_0 - \frac{\Delta m}{\Delta t} \cdot t)$$

we get to:

$$dv = \frac{\Delta m}{\Delta t}v' \left(\frac{1 - \frac{m_0 g}{\frac{\Delta m}{\Delta t}v'}}{m_0 - \frac{\Delta m}{\Delta t}t} \right) \cdot dt \quad \text{or}$$

$$dv = v'\left(1 - \frac{m_0 g}{m_0 - \frac{\Delta m}{\Delta t}v'}\right) \cdot \frac{\frac{\Delta m}{\Delta t}dt}{m_0 - \frac{\Delta m}{\Delta t}t},$$

we integrate speed $d\upsilon$ from 0 to u and time from 0 to t

$$\int_0^\upsilon d\upsilon = \upsilon' \left(1 - \frac{m_0 g}{\frac{\Delta m}{\Delta t}\upsilon'} \right) \int_0^t \frac{\frac{\Delta m}{\Delta t}}{m_0 - \frac{\Delta m}{\Delta t}t} \cdot dt,$$

from this

$$\upsilon = \upsilon' \left(1 - \frac{m_0 g}{\frac{\Delta m}{\Delta t}\upsilon'} \right) \ln \frac{m_0}{m_0 - \frac{\Delta m}{\Delta t}t}.$$

We calculate:

$$\upsilon = 800\frac{m}{c}\left(1 - \frac{1{,}2\text{кг} \cdot 9{,}81\frac{m}{c^2}}{0{,}4\frac{\text{кг}}{c} \cdot 800\frac{m}{c}} \right) \ln \frac{1{,}2\text{кг}}{1{,}2\text{кг} - 0{,}4\frac{\text{кг}}{c} \cdot 1c} = 800\frac{m}{c}(1 - 0{,}037)\ln\frac{3}{2} = 308{,}16\frac{m}{c}$$

Answer: $\upsilon = 308{,}16\frac{m}{c}$

Issues for independent solution

A load of mass 1 kg is hanging on a string. If the loaded rope is raised with an acceleration of a) 5 m/s2; b) Find the tension in the string if it is lowered with an acceleration of 5 m/s2.

An aerostat of mass m together with ballast is descending with a constant acceleration a. How much ballast must be dropped from the aerostat in order to make it fall with a vertical upward acceleration of the same volume as the previous one? Ignore friction.

Assuming that the acceleration of the elevators of the Ostankino television tower is constant in value, and the same during the start of movement and braking, find the pressure force exerted on the bottom of the elevator at the beginning, in the middle and at the end of the rise of the 100 kg load. It is known that the elevator rises to a height of 337 m in 60 seconds, and its maximum speed is 7 m/s.

Two scales were connected by a string and passed through a weightless block. The stones move with an acceleration of 3.27m/s2. If it is known that the tension force of the string is 13 N, determine the mass of the stones. Ignore friction on the block.

A car with a mass of 1000 kg during movement is affected by a frictional force equal to 0.1 part of its weight. What must be the thrust of the car engine so that the car moves with a uniform acceleration of 2 m/s2.

Determine the tension force at the bottom point of the circle in the horizontal movement of a 0.1 kg ball on the rod in the vertical plane, and the tension force at the top point of 2N.

A car with a mass of 10 kg is moving along a concave bridge with a radius of curvature of 100 m. What force does the car exert on the bridge when it moves at a speed of 15 m/s at the bottom point?

If the turning radius is 25 m, at what maximum speed can the motorcycle turn on a horizontal plane with a coefficient of friction of 0.4.

A pilot with a mass of 80 kg performed a Nesterov maneuver with a radius of 250 m. The speed of the plane was 140 m/s. How much force does the pilot press on the seat at the bottom of the ramp?

10. Determine the tension force at the upper point of 2N at the lower point of the circle when a 0.1 kg ball moves smoothly in a vertical plane on the rod.

A car with a mass of 10 kg is moving along a concave bridge with a radius of curvature of 100 m. What force does the car exert on the bridge when it moves at a speed of 15 m/s at the bottom point?

CHAPTER III
FORCES IN NATURE

3.1. The whole universe is the law of gravity

In 1665, Isaac Newton used the laws of dynamics to create the universal law of gravitation. The law of universal gravitation is defined as follows: All objects in the universe interact with each other with a force that is proportional to the product of their masses and inversely proportional to the square of the distance between them. The forces of attraction between all objects in nature are called gravitational forces

$$F = G \frac{M \cdot m}{r^2}. \qquad (3.1)$$

Here G is the gravitational constant

$$G = \gamma = 6,67 \cdot 10^{-11} \frac{H \cdot м^2}{кг^2}$$

The meaning of the gravitational constant in the law of universal gravitation is as follows: a quantity equal to the force of attraction between two bodies with a mass of more than 1 kg and a distance between them of 1 m. If it is, it is M=m=1 кг, r=1 м, and it is called the gravitational constant $\gamma = F$. The gravitational constant was determined experimentally by Henry

G. Cavendish
(1731-1810)

Cavendish in 1978 and its value is $\gamma = 6.67 \cdot 10^{-11} \dfrac{\text{Н} \cdot \text{м}^2}{\text{кг}^2}$

In the law of universal gravitation, interacting bodies are considered material points. For example, consider the interactions between the Sun and other planets. If we do not consider bodies as material points, then to calculate the effect of gravity, each body is mentally divided into elementary parts, and for every two elementary parts, the whole universe is calculated by the formula of the law of gravity, and then it is found by adding the forces geometrically. Gravitational forces do not depend on the environment in which objects are located (in air, liquid, space). The universal law of gravitation does not answer the question of how the interaction between bodies takes place. This question is answered by thinking as follows. The interaction between bodies is carried out through the gravitational field. It has been found that around each body there is an invisible gravitational field called the gravity field. These fields are created by objects. The gravitational field around an object is uniform, it is stronger near the object and gradually weakens as it moves away from it. One of the main properties of gravity or a gravitational field is that when any material point of mass m is introduced into the field, a gravitational force F is exerted proportional to this mass

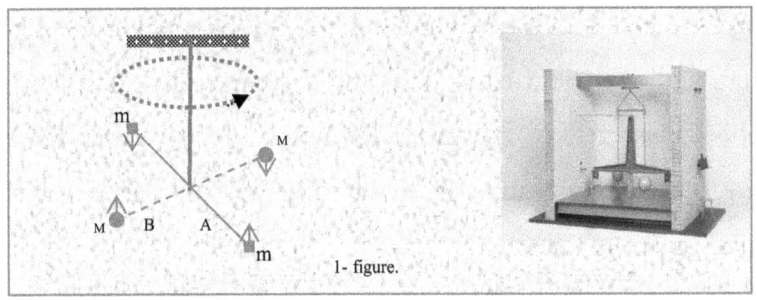

1- figure.

$F = mG$. (3.2)

In order to know the quantitative characteristics of the gravitational field, a physical quantity called the field strength is introduced. Field strength is numerically equal to the force exerted by the field on a material point of unit mass

$$G = \frac{F}{m}.$$

The field strength represents the strength characteristic of the gravitational field. If the intensity of the field is the same at all points, the field is said to be uniform. Using the universal gravitation formula $G = \frac{F}{m}$, we write

$$G = \frac{\gamma \cdot \frac{M \cdot m}{r^2}}{m} = \gamma \cdot \frac{M}{r^2}. \qquad (3.3)$$

As can be seen from this formula, the strength of the field depends on the mass of the body creating the field and the distance from this body to a certain point of the field. The strength of the field does not depend on the mass of the body being introduced into the gravitational field. Now let's consider the gravitational field created by the system of fixed material points of mass m1, m2, ... mn. The force exerted by the m-mass of the system on a material point of mass m placed at an arbitrary point of the field

$$F_1 = \gamma \cdot \frac{m \cdot m}{r^2} = m \cdot G_1 \qquad (3.4)$$

where G1 is the strength of the field creating a material point at the point where the body of mass m is placed. The equivalent force of the forces acting on the material point of mass m by the material points in the system is equal to the vector sum of the forces

$$F_1 = \sum_{i=1}^{n} F_i = m \sum_{i=1}^{n} G_i \qquad (3.5)$$

or

$$\vec{F} = m \cdot \vec{G}$$

in this $G = \sum_{i=1}^{n} G_i$ the gravitational field strength of the system of material points. Thus, in the combination of several gravitational fields, the strength of this resultant field is equal to the vector sum of the strengths of all the joining gravitational fields. This is called the principle of superposition of fields. Mass is the source of gravitational forces. Inert and gravitational masses are equal to each other. Gravitational force cannot be lost or reduced by any obstacle. Gravity of a body to the Earth is a special case of the manifestation of gravity.

3.2. Kepler's laws

The fall of objects to the Earth, the oscillation of a pendulum, the laws of motion of planets and satellites and other examples

Kepler (1571-1630)

testify to the existence of gravitational forces between objects. Using the results of the observations of the great astronomer Tycho Brahe, the German scientist Johann Kepler empirically discovered the laws of motion of the planets. Since ancient times, people have noticed that the positions of the stars in the sky relative to each other do not change over long periods of time, and the planets move in complex trajectories between them. The ancient Greek scientist Ptolemy founded the geocentric theory, which means that all the planets move around the earth. Beruni was a supporter of the same idea. Great scholars such as Ahmad al-Farghani, Ulug'bek, Ali Kushchi also performed extensive work on determining the position of stars and planets. Geocentric idea at the beginning of the 16th century N. He reigned until Copernicus founded the heliocentric system. Long astronomical observations showed that Copernicus' heliocentric system was correct. 1. Kepler's first law. Action in the central force field.

A material point moving in a central force field constitutes a conservative system because it is an external field potential and a stationary field. Therefore, in the movement of a material point, not only its angular momentum is stored, but also the mechanical energy of the point

$W = W_k + W_n = \text{const}$.

The kinetic energy of a material point can be expressed in the following form

$$W_k = \frac{m\upsilon^2}{2} = \frac{m}{2}\left(\upsilon_r^2 + \upsilon_\phi^2\right) = \frac{m}{2}\left[\left(\frac{dr}{dt}\right)^2 + \left(r\frac{d\phi}{dt}\right)^2\right] = \frac{m}{2}\left[\left(\frac{dr}{dt}\right)^2 + \left(\frac{L}{mr}\right)^2\right]$$

Substituting this expression for Wk into (3.6) and solving for $\dfrac{dr}{dt}$

$$\frac{dr}{dt} = \sqrt{\frac{2}{m}(W - W_n) - \left(\frac{L}{mr}\right)^2}$$

we get the result. from (3.6).

$$\frac{d\phi}{dt} = \frac{L}{mr^2}$$

it turns out to be. so that

$$d\phi = \frac{L/r^2}{\sqrt{2m(W-W_n)-(L/r)^2}}dr,$$

$$\phi = -\int \frac{d(L/r)}{\sqrt{2m(W-W_n)-(L/r)^2}}$$

will be To find this integral, it is necessary to know the exact representation of the relationship between the potential energy Wn and r. For a material point, the movement in the central field is of great practical importance

$$F_r = \frac{\beta}{r^2}; \qquad W_n = \frac{\beta}{r},$$

here β=const. W_n we put this expression of in (3.7).

$$\phi = -\int \frac{d(L/r)}{\sqrt{2mW - 2m\beta/r - (L/r)^2}} = -\int \frac{d(L/r + m\beta/L)}{\sqrt{[2mW+(m\beta/L)^2]-[L/r+m\beta/L]^2}}$$

If

$$\frac{L}{r} + \frac{m\beta}{L} = \eta, \qquad 2mW + \left(\frac{m\beta}{L}\right)^2 = a^2,$$

if we enter the designations, the last integral will look like in the table

$$\beta = -\int \frac{d\eta}{\sqrt{a^2-\eta^2}} = \arccos\frac{\eta}{a} + \phi_0,$$

here φ_0 – the constant of integration can be converted to zero when $\varphi=0$, taking the angle $\eta=a$ as the starting point. Putting the expressions of η and a in (3.8), we get the trajectory equation of the material point

$$\varphi = \arccos \frac{L/r + m\beta/L}{\sqrt{2mW + (m\beta/L)^2}}$$

or

$$r = \frac{L}{-m\beta/L + \cos\varphi\sqrt{2mW + (m\beta/L)^2}}.$$

If a material point is attracted to the center of forces, such as the planets in the central gravitational field of the Sun, then $\beta<0$ and the point trajectory formula

$$r = \frac{Đ}{1 + å\cos\varphi}$$

can be written in the form, here

$$P = \frac{L^2}{m|\beta|}, \quad e = \sqrt{\frac{2WL^2}{m\beta^2} + 1}.$$

The trajectory of a material point represents a curve of the second order, where P is the focal parameter of the curve, and ε is the eccentricity. The following possible types of material point trajectory can be:

a) elliptical orbit when W<0 (e<1);

b) parabolic orbit when W=0 (e=1);

c) hyperbolic orbit when W>0 (e>1);

g) A straight line trajectory passing through the center of forces when L=0 (R=0, ε=1).

In the first three cases, the center of force coincides with one of the foci of the orbit. For planets moving in the Sun's gravitational field, W<0, so Kepler's first law applies to them: all planets in the Solar System move in elliptical orbits with the Sun at one focus.

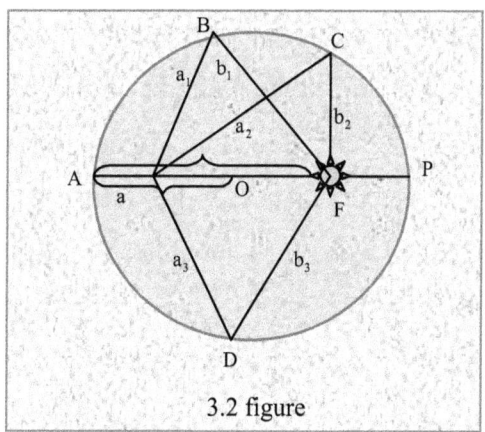

3.2 figure

2. Kepler's second law

We explain the motion characteristics of a material point in the field of central forces and, in particular, the laws of motion of the planets in the solar system along their orbits around the Sun. To a point on the field

$$\vec{F} = F_r(r)\frac{\vec{r}}{r} \qquad (3.12)$$

is affected by the central force, where r is the radius vector of the material point, which is passed through the coordinate origin 0, which coincides with the center of force. The moment M of the central forces relative to the center of force 0 is exactly zero

$$\vec{M} = [\vec{r} \cdot \vec{F}] = \frac{\vec{F}_r(r)}{r}[\vec{r} \cdot \vec{r}] = 0. \qquad (3.13)$$

So, according to (3.13), the moment of momentum of a material point relative to the center of force does not change during its movement

$$\vec{L} = [m\vec{r} \cdot \vec{v}] = \text{const}, \qquad (3.14)$$

where m and v are the mass and velocity of the material point. The vector L is always orthogonal to the plane of vectors r and y. Therefore, the constancy of the direction of the vector L indicates that the movement of the material point in the central force field is flat. The speed of a point can be divided into radial and transversal components

$$\vec{L} = m[\vec{r} \cdot \vec{V}_r] + m[\vec{r} \cdot \vec{V}_\phi] = m[\vec{r} \cdot \vec{V}_\phi],$$
$$\vec{L} = m[\vec{r} \cdot \vec{v}_\phi] = mr^2 \frac{d\phi}{dt} = 2m\sigma \qquad (3.15)$$

will be Here r and φ are the polar coordinates of the point (see Fig. 3.3); σ is its sectoral speed. So,.

$$\vec{L} = m[\vec{r} \cdot \vec{V}] = \text{const}$$

The following law follows from this: In the movement of a material point in the field of central forces, its sectoral speed remains constant.

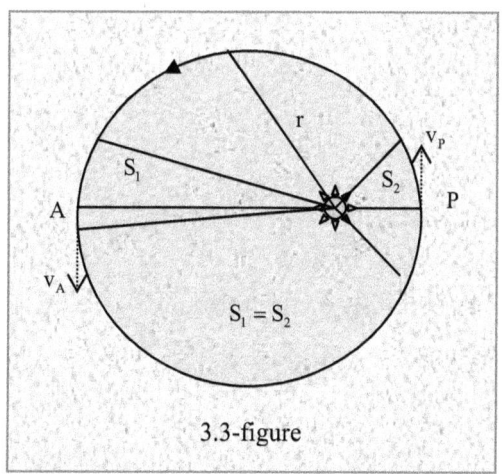

3.3-figure

(The radius vector transferred from the Sun to the planet passes the same surfaces at the same time intervals (Fig. 3.3)). For the first time this law I. It was determined by Kepler (1609) in accordance with the movement of the planets in the central gravitational field of the Sun. It is called Kepler's second law.

3. Kepler's third law

According to Kepler's second law, the sectorial speed σ of each planet is constant. So, the period of rotation of the planet in its orbit is equal to the ratio of the surface bounded by its orbit to its sectorial speed σ

$$T = \frac{C}{\sigma}$$

The surface of an ellipse $C = \pi a b$, where a and b are its major and minor semi-axes. In this

$$b = a\sqrt{1-e^2}, \quad P = a(1-e^2) \qquad (3.17)$$

that is, and using relation (3.17),

$$T^2 = \frac{L^2}{4m^2}\pi^2 P a^3 \qquad (3.18)$$

we get the result. (3.17) according to the formula

$$P = \frac{L^2}{m|\beta|},$$

where M is the mass of the Sun

$$T^2 = \frac{4\pi^2}{GM}a^3$$

the formula is derived. Equation (3.19) expresses Kepler's third law: the squares of the periods of rotation of the planets around the Sun are directly proportional to the cubes of the semi-major axes of their orbits. $\beta>0$ when a material point is pushed away from the center of force (for example, in

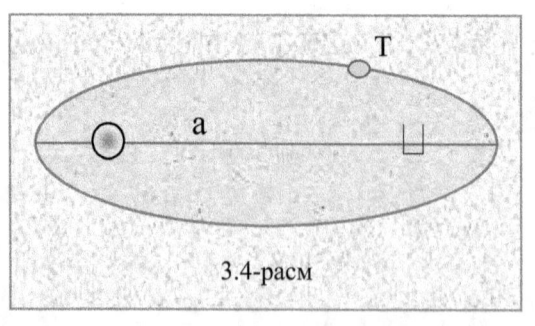

3.4-расм

the movement of a point electric charge q in the field of a fixed charge q of the same sign as it).

$$r = \frac{p}{-1 + e\cos j},$$

where r and e are determined by the formula (3.17). The total energy of a material point

$$W = (W_k + W_n) > 0,$$

because Therefore, W>1 and the material point moves in the field of repulsive central forces either along a hyperbolic orbit, or (when L=0) along a straight line passing through the center of forces.

Natural forces

In nature, forces are diverse in nature, but in mechanics, these forces are divided into groups.

1) Elastic forces
2) Frictional forces
3) Gravitational forces

3.4.1. Elastic forces

Elastic force is a force that occurs as a result of body deformation and returns the deformed body to its original motion.

Under the influence of an external force, a solid body is of two types depending on its shape or size.

1) elastic deformation
2) plastic deformation

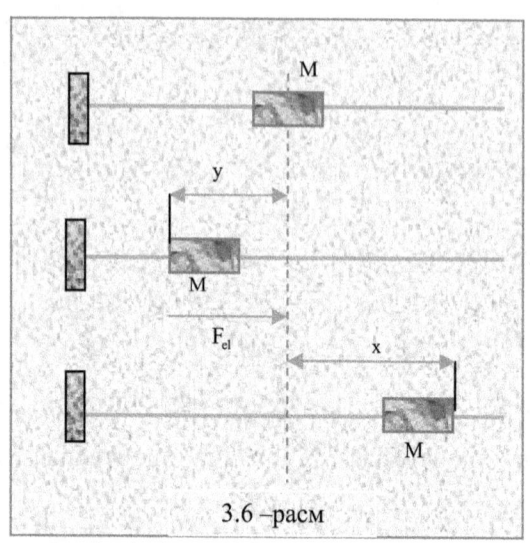

3.6 –расм

When the body does not return to its original position after the external force stops, it is called elastic deformation. If the deformation does not disappear even after the external force stops, it is called plastic deformation. The elastic force is opposed to the direction of displacement of the deformation vector of the particles of the body, which is perpendicular to the contact surface of the interacting bodies. English physicist Robert Hooke, a colleague of Newton, studied elastic deformation and created Hooke's law .

$$F_{эл} = -кx \qquad (3.23)$$

It is a mathematical expression of Hooke's law, where - elastic force x is the deformation distance, k is the proportionality coefficient, which shows the uniformity of the body depending on the material and size of the body. Hooke's law is defined as follows: The elastic force arising in the deformation of the body is proportional to the elongation of the body and is opposite to the displacement of the particles of the body relative to other particles. Mechanical stress refers to the force acting vertically on the unit face of the rod and is denoted by the letter - (sigma).

$$\sigma = \frac{F}{S} \qquad (3.24)$$

Relative elongation of the sturgeon

$$E = \frac{\Delta \ell}{\ell_o} = \frac{\ell - \ell_o}{\ell_o} \qquad (3.25)$$

In this: ℓ_o - initial length ℓ - next length, $D\ell = \ell - \ell_o$ - absolute elongation, E – relative elongation. During the deformation, if the rod is stretched, E>0, if it is compressed, E<0, that is, it is stretched accordingly and compression deformations take place. Mechanical stress is proportional to relative elongation.

$$\sigma = \varepsilon \times E \qquad (3.26)$$

in which: ε - is the coefficient of proportionality, which is the Young's modulus (called the modulus of elasticity.) from the expression (3.23) and (3.26)

$$\varepsilon = \frac{\sigma}{E} = \frac{\sigma}{\frac{\Delta l}{l_o}} \qquad (3.27)$$

resulting from this

$$\varepsilon = \frac{F \times l_0}{S \times D1} \qquad (3.28)$$

originates.

3.4.2. Frictional forces

Frictional forces appear when bodies or parts of bodies move relative to each other. Friction: 1) External, 2) Internal friction. Friction that occurs as a result of two objects moving relative to each other when they are in contact is called external friction. The friction between the liquid or gas particles of the body is called internal friction. External friction:

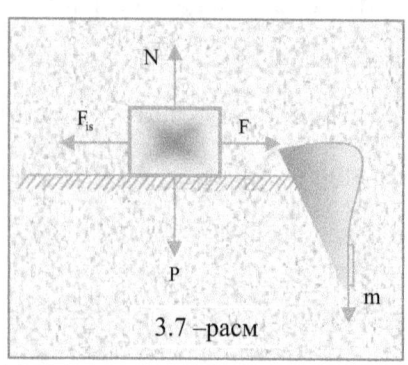

3.7 –расм

1) Friction at rest
2) Sliding friction
3) Rolling friction is divided into.

As the frictional force is directed along the frictional surfaces, it prevents the surfaces from moving, as a result, the body heats up and the energy of the body decreases. The force of friction at rest is proportional to the force of pressure.

$$\vec{F}_{is} \, \mu \, \vec{P}$$

$\vec{F}_{is}$ – friction force, $\vec{P}$ – pressure force, $\vec{N}$ – reaction force.

Newton's third law basically $\vec{P} = \vec{N}$ is equal to. Friction at rest keeps bodies in a state of relative rest. At the base, it causes the body to accelerate in motion. When the external force acting on the body is greater than the maximum frictional force at rest, the body begins to slide, that is, sliding friction occurs. The laws of sliding friction were developed by French physicists G. Amonton and Sh. Discovered by Coulomb. The maximum value of the frictional force at rest is proportional

Usually always µ<1. The frictional force in rolling is much smaller than the frictional force in sliding. The force of rolling friction is inversely proportional to the radius of the rolling object

$$\vec{F}_д = \mu_д \times \frac{\vec{N}}{R}$$

(3.31)

will be equal to Here: Fd is the force of rolling friction, ☐d is the coefficient of rolling friction, R is the radius of the rolling body. Friction depends on the speed of movement of the body and the temperature of the body. With increasing speed, friction decreases, and with increasing temperature, friction increases.

3.4.3. Gravity

All objects near the surface of the earth fall to the ground with the same acceleration due to the gravity of the earth. This acceleration is the acceleration of free fall, it $g \approx 9.8\frac{M}{c^2}$ is equal to. To any body in number systems related to the earth

$$\overset{\text{®}}{P} = m\overset{\text{®}}{g} \qquad (3.32)$$

force affects. This force is called gravity. The difference between the force of gravity and the force of gravity is 0.36%, and since this difference is small, it can be considered equal to the force of gravity on the earth. Acceleration of an object in free fall according to Newton's second law

$$\overset{\text{®}}{g} = \frac{\overset{\text{®}}{P}}{m} = \frac{\overset{\text{®}}{F}}{m} = g\frac{mM}{R^2 m} = g\frac{M_{ep}}{R^2} \qquad (3.33)$$

will be equal to. For an object at a height h above the ground

$$g_h = g\frac{M}{(R+h)^2} \qquad (3.34)$$

is the force of gravity

$$P_h = mg_h = g\frac{m \times M_{ep}}{(R_{ep} + h)^2} \qquad (3.35)$$

will be equal to.

When a body hangs on a support or suspension, it is at rest relative to the ground, where the force of gravity is balanced by the reaction force of the support or suspension. Due to gravity, the body is balanced. The force exerted by a body on a suspension or a support due to its gravity is called body weight.

$\overset{\text{®}}{P} = m\overset{\text{®}}{g}$, (3.36)

$\overset{\text{®}}{P}$ – body weight or weight. The weight of the body is applied to the support or suspension, and the force of gravity is exerted on the body, which is a scalar quantity. At rest, the weight of an object is equal to the force of gravity. If the support or suspension moves with acceleration relative to the ground, the weight of the object is different from the force of gravity. If an object moves upward in a direction perpendicular to the acceleration of free fall, its weight in motion

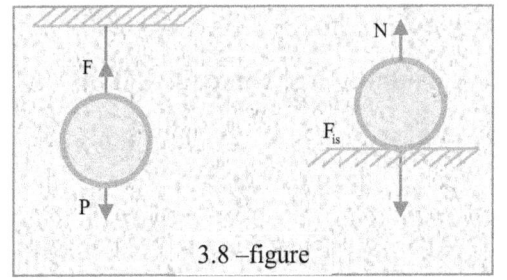

3.8 –figure

P=m(g - a) (3.37)

is equal to and is less than the weight at rest. If the body moves downward with the same acceleration, its weight in motion

P=m(g+a) (3.38)

is equal to and is heavier than the weight in peace. If the body falls freely with support and suspension, then a=g,

P=m(g - a)=m(g-g)=O (3.39)

is, the weight of the body is lost, and the body is in the state of weight. Weightlessness is a state in which the weight of the body is equal to zero. In the case of weightlessness, only the force of gravity acts on the body, and the force gives the body an acceleration g. In the state of weightlessness, the body does not undergo deformation. The state of weightlessness is manifested when the spacecraft turns off its engine and moves around the earth.

3.5. Motion of bodies of variable mass. Reactive action

When we say a variable mass body, we mean a body whose mass changes during its movement, that is, its mass can decrease or increase, obeying the laws of classical mechanics. For example, on summer days, as a result of cars spraying water on the street, rockets and jets burning fuel, their mass decreases. As a result of the fall of various meteorites on the earth, the mass of the earth increases and so on. But in this case, we assume that the mass does not change with the increase in speed. Generalizing Newton's second law for these cases,

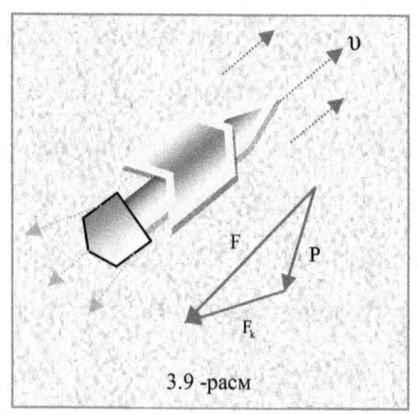

3.9 -расм

$$\vec{F} = \frac{d\vec{P}}{dt} = \frac{d(m\vec{\vartheta})}{dt} = \vec{\vartheta}\frac{dm}{dt} + m\frac{d\vec{\vartheta}}{dt} = \vec{\vartheta}\frac{dm}{dt} + m\vec{a}$$

(3.40)

will be It can be seen from formula (3.40) that with a change in mass, the magnitude of the speed also changes, in general, it does not coincide with the direction of the force, and the correct proportionality of the speed to the force is not preserved.

EXAMPLES OF PROBLEM SOLVING

Issue 1. How many times faster does the earth have to rotate so that objects at the equator are weightless?

Given: $g = 9,8$ м/с^2, $R=6,38\cdot 10^6$ м, $T=24$ соат$=864\cdot 10^2$ с.

Need to find: $v_2/v_1=?$

Solution: ернинг ўз ўқи атрофида айланиш тезлиги:

$$\vartheta_1 = \frac{2\pi R}{T},$$

where R, T are the Earth's radius and rotation period. In order for the body to be weightless at the equator, the centrifugal force of inertia must be equal to the force of gravity:

$$\frac{m\vartheta^2}{R} = mg$$

Ratios of (1) and (2).

$$\frac{\vartheta_2}{\vartheta_1} = \frac{T}{2\pi}\sqrt{\frac{g}{R}}.$$

we get and calculate:

$$\frac{\vartheta_2}{\vartheta_1} = \frac{864 \cdot 10^2 с}{6,28}\sqrt{\frac{9,8 \, m/с^2}{6,38 \cdot 10^6 \, m}} = 17 \text{ marta.}$$

Answer: $\vartheta_2/\vartheta_1 = 17$ times.

Issue 2. Find the numerical values of the first and second space velocities of the object thrown from the ground.

Given: m=5,98·10²⁴ кг, R=6400 км, G=6,67·10⁻¹¹ H·м²/кг².

Need to find : $\vartheta_1 = ?$ $\vartheta_2 = ?$

Solution: 1) Let's say that the body is at some very small height above the surface of the earth: when the body is given a certain speed in the horizontal direction, the body turns into a satellite of the earth and begins to move around the earth in a circular orbit (we assume that there is no air resistance). The velocity at this time is called the first cosmic velocity. The size of an object moving along a circular orbit

$$F_M = \frac{m\vartheta_1^2}{R}$$

the center is affected by a force of attraction. Here m is the mass of the object, y1 is the speed of movement, R is the radius of curvature of the trajectory. In this case, the gravitational force of the earth is the centripetal force. This is the pull force:

$$F_T = G\frac{mM}{R^2}$$

is represented by the formula. Here M is the mass of the earth, G is the gravitational constant, R is the distance of the body from the center of the earth (equal to the radius of curvature of the trajectory). Equating the expression of the centripetal force FM to the expression of the gravitational force F:

$$\frac{m\vartheta_1^2}{R} = G\frac{mM}{R^2}$$

we form the equation From this:

$$\vartheta_1 = \sqrt{G\frac{M}{R}}\;.$$

We calculate:

$$\vartheta_1 = \sqrt{\frac{6,67\cdot 10^{-11}\cdot 5,96\cdot 10^{24}}{6,4\cdot 10^6}} = 7,9 \text{ km/ñ}.$$

υ_1 can be found even if the mass of the earth is unknown. To do this, we divide both parts of equation (2) by m:

$$\frac{F_T}{m} = G\frac{M}{R^2}\;.$$

According to Newton's second law, the acceleration of a free-falling body on the surface of the earth in the ratio FT/m is equal to g:

$$g = \frac{GM}{R^2}$$

So,

$$\frac{GM}{R} = gR$$

and

$$\vartheta_1 = \sqrt{gR}.$$

(ϑ_1 divide both sides of equation (1) by m to find). If we put numerical values in the formula (4), we get the same $\vartheta = 7.9$ km/s. We use the law of conservation of energy to find the second cosmic velocity. The work required to throw an object an infinite distance from the surface of the earth is equal to the kinetic energy of this object:

$$A = W_k, \quad W_k = \frac{m\vartheta^2}{2}.$$

When calculating the work done to throw an object from the surface of the earth to infinity, it is necessary to pay attention to the fact that the acting force is a variable quantity. Therefore, we divide the distance into such infinitesimal pieces dr that the force is assumed to be constant over this distance. Then elementary work:

$$dA = F\,dr.$$

This is due to the law of universal gravitation

$$F = G\frac{mM}{r^2}$$

we put:

$$dA = F \cdot dr = G\frac{mM}{r^2} \cdot dr.$$

We integrate this expression over the distance from the earth's surface r=R to infinity:

$$A = GmM \int_{r=R}^{r=\infty} \frac{dr}{r^2},$$

but

$$\int_{r=R}^{r=\infty} \frac{dr}{r} = -\frac{1}{r}\Big|_{R}^{\infty} = \frac{1}{R}.$$

Hence, the work done to throw an object from the surface of the earth to infinity is:

$$A = G\frac{mM}{R}.$$

so that

$$\frac{m\vartheta^2}{2} = G\frac{mM}{R},$$

from this:

$$\vartheta = \vartheta_2 = \sqrt{2G\frac{M}{R}}$$

the second cosmic velocity formula is derived.
We calculate:

$$\vartheta_2 = \sqrt{\frac{2 \cdot 6,67 \cdot 10^{-11} \text{H} \cdot \text{м}^2/\text{кг}^2 \cdot 5,98 \cdot 10^{24}\text{кг}}{6,4 \cdot 10^6 \text{ь}}} = 11,16\frac{\text{км}}{\text{с}}.$$

Answer: $v_1 = 7{,}9$ км/с;

Issue 3. On December 2, 1976, the Molniya-2 communication satellite was launched into an elliptical orbit with an apogee of 40,608 km and a perigee of 657 km. Find the period of rotation of the moon around the earth and the ratio of the speed at perigee to the speed at apogee, as well as the ratio of kinetic and total energies (Fig. 1).

Given: $h_1 = 657$ км, $h_2 = 40608$ км

Need to find:

$T = ?$ $\dfrac{v_p}{v_a} = ?$ $\dfrac{K_p}{K_a} = ?$

Solution: we apply Kepler's third law for the rotation of "Molniya-2" and the moon around the earth.

$$\frac{T_2^2}{T_1^2} = \frac{a_2^3}{a_1^3},$$

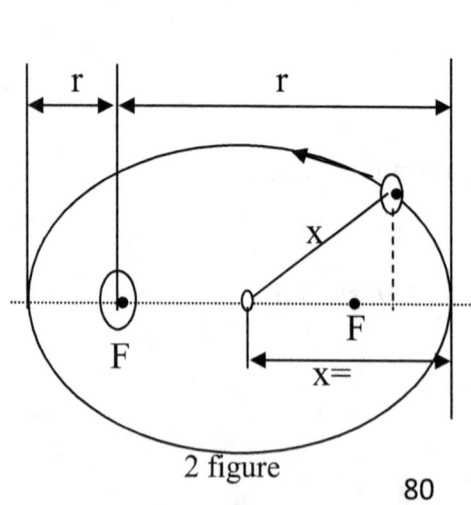

2 figure

where T1, T2 are respectively the rotation periods of the Moon and "Molniya-2" around the Earth; 1 - the distance between the centers of the Earth and the Moon; 2 – the average distance between the earth and the centers of "Molniya-2". For the Moon, T1=27.3 days= 655.2 hours and the distance from the Earth to the Moon as the semi-major axis of the Moon's orbit can be taken as ρ=384000 km. But if the radii of the Earth and the Moon are also taken into account, the problem will be solved more clearly

$a_1 = r + R + r_{ой} = (384 + 6{,}37 + 1{,}74) \cdot 10^3$ km $= 392 \cdot 10^3$ km,

where R and roy are the radii of the Earth and the Moon, respectively. For the companion

$a_2 = 0{,}5 \ (2R + h_1 + h_2) = 0{,}5 \ (2 \cdot 6370 + 657 + 40608) = 27000$ km.

Thus, the rotation period of "Molniya-2":

$$T_2 = T_1 \frac{a_2}{a_1} \sqrt{\frac{a_2}{a_1}} = 655{,}2 \, соат \cdot \frac{27000 \, км}{392000 \, км} \sqrt{\frac{27000 \, км}{392000 \, км}} = 12{,}15 \, соат$$

We find the ratio of the satellite's speed at perigee to its speed at apogee from the law of conservation of momentum:

$m\vartheta_n r_n = m\vartheta_a r_a$

in this

$$\frac{\vartheta_n}{\vartheta_a} = \frac{r_a}{r_n}.$$

But $r_a = a + \varepsilon x$ and $r_n = a - \varepsilon x$, in this a – semimajor axis of the ellipse, $\varepsilon = \frac{c}{a} = \frac{F_1 \cdot F_2}{2a}$ - the eccentricity of the ellipse, x – is the satellite abscissa, the largest value of which is x=a (Fig. 1).

$F_1 \cdot F_2 = r_a - r_н = 40608$ км $- 657$ км $= 39951$ км,

$$\varepsilon = \frac{F_1 \cdot F_2}{2a} = \frac{39951}{2(40608 + 6370)} = 0,425.$$

So,

$$\frac{\vartheta_n}{\vartheta_a} = \frac{a + \varepsilon a}{a - \varepsilon a} = \frac{1 + \varepsilon}{1 - \varepsilon} = \frac{1 + 0,425}{1 - 0,425} \approx 2,5.$$

The ratio of energies of "Molniya-2" in the apagee and perigee states:

$$n = \frac{K_n}{K_a} = \left(\frac{\vartheta_n}{\vartheta_a}\right)^2 = \left(\frac{1,425}{0,575}\right)^2 = (2,5)^2 = 6,25.$$

Answer: $T_2 = 12,15$ hour; $\frac{\vartheta_n}{\vartheta_a} = 2.5$; $\frac{K_n}{K_a} = 6.25$.

CHAPTER IV
WORK, ENERGY AND POWER

We looked at the concept of momentum of a body above. Impulse can be considered as a specific measure of the mechanical movement of an object. But such a dynamic description of the body cannot be a universal measure for all forms of movement. We will see this in the following examples. If we observe an inelastic collision of two identical plate balls moving against each other, the balls are in motion until the collision, and after the collision they are at rest. In these cases, the law of conservation of momentum is fulfilled: the sum of the momentum of the balls before the collision is zero, and it is also zero after the collision. But the balls were in motion before impact and at rest after impact. If we consider momentum as a universal measure of motion, then we will come to the wrong conclusion that the spheres with motion lose their motion. If we measure the temperature of the balls before and after the impact, we see that the temperature rises. In this case, the mechanical movement of the spheres is not lost, it becomes the molecular movement of the substance. So, momentum cannot be a universal measure in all cases of mechanical movement. As a result of the friction of objects, mechanical movement is lost and turns into heat. Now let's observe the motion of a body moving in a straight line. Due to the presence of friction between the bodies, the bodies heat up, that is, the mechanical movement of the bodies turns into the chaotic heat movement of the molecules that make up these bodies. But the momentum of the body remains unchanged in straight line motion, but it does not describe the amount of heat released. Thus, mechanical motion does not disappear, but matter is transferred to other forms of motion. Hence, there must be a new physical quantity as a general measure of motion patterns. Such a physical quantity is energy. Energy is a universal quantitative measure of the motion of matter in any form. To determine the state of mechanical movement of a system of bodies, it is enough to know their relative location and speed, to describe the state of a gas, it is necessary to know its volume, temperature and pressure. Energy is a function of the state of the system.

4.1. Work and power

The exchange of mechanical motion between bodies or the transition of mechanical motion to other forms of motion occurs as a result of the interaction of bodies.

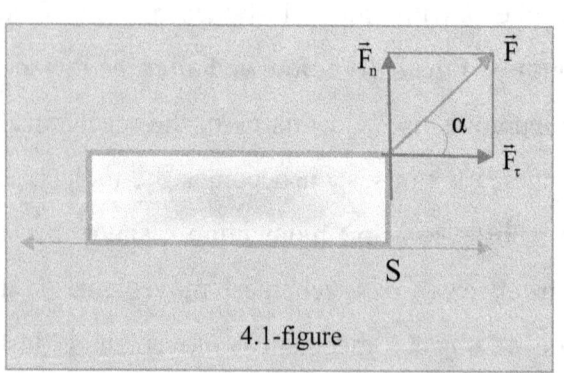

4.1-figure

Movement is transferred from one body to another as a result of bodies interacting with each other. It is known that the interaction takes place through force, that is, the mechanical behavior of the body changes under the influence of force, but it should also be taken into account that if the body is at rest, then it cannot be concluded that no force acts on it: in fact, the forces acting on the body are the same -try to balance one. For example, the force of gravity of an object standing still on a table is balanced by the reaction force of the table on this object. In some cases, the action of an external force is associated with motion, and due to this motion, the object travels a certain distance in a certain time interval - it does work. The concept of work used in our daily life and the concept of work related to mechanical movement are fundamentally different from each other; the difference is that mechanical work is related to motion and is measured by the work done by an external force in moving objects from one place to another.

Experiments show that the magnitude of the movement in such processes is equal to the force multiplied by the magnitude of displacement. This resulting physical quantity is called work. In other words, the change of energy is called work. Work is a scalar quantity

$A = F \cdot S \cos \alpha$

S – displacement or distance, F – force, $\cos \alpha$ – the angle between the direction of the force and the distance. In the international system of units, the unit of work is the work done when moving bodies in the direction of force for a distance of one meter under the influence of one newton. The unit of this work (Joule) is J=N·m. Therefore, work is a measure of the transfer of motion from one body to another, or a measure of the transfer of energy from one body to another. If a material point moves a distance S under the influence of a constant force F (Fig. 4.1), then the work done by the force

$$A = F_\tau \cdot S.$$

Here, F is the projection of force F in the direction of displacement,

$$F_\tau = F \cdot \cos\alpha.$$

It will look like Figure 4.1. α is the angle between the direction of movement of the body and the force F, taking into account (4.2), we write (4.1) as follows:

$$A = F \cdot S \cos\alpha$$

1. If the angle between the direction of force and the direction of displacement is $\alpha<90°$, then $\cos\alpha>0$. So, the force does positive work (A>0). The body is in forward motion;
2. If $\alpha>90°$, then $\cos\alpha<0$. In this case, force does negative work. For example, friction force and braking force;
3. If the force direction is perpendicular to the displacement, $\alpha=90°$, then $\cos\alpha=0$. Therefore, the work done by the force is

zero, that is, no energy is transferred.

In order to better visualize the positive or negative performance of the work, we give the following example. When a body is moving under the influence of a force, the force of friction, which resists the movement, acts simultaneously with this force. This force is directed in the direction opposite to the direction of motion, so the work done by it is negative. If an object is moving in a straight line with constant velocity under the influence of a force, then according to Newton's first law, no external force acts on the object and the work done is zero. But in fact, when an object moves along a straight line with constant speed, the external force is used only to balance the frictional force, and that force is numerically equal to the frictional force. For example, when a car is moving in a straight line with constant speed, the thrust of the engine is balanced by the frictional force, so the work done by it is positive. If the car's engine is turned off, it will stop after traveling a certain distance, and for this distance, only friction and air resistance will act on it, and the work done by the force will be negative. It follows from here that the work done by the force opposing the motion of the body is always negative. If the magnitude of the force is variable at a certain distance, then to calculate the work done, we divide the distance into elementary displacements, and in these elementary displacements, we can consider the force as a constant quantity (Fig. 4.2). If we calculate the elementary work done in each elementary displacement, and then take the algebraic sum of these elementary works, then the work done by the variable force F at a distance S is expressed as follows

$$A = \sum_{i=1}^{n} \Delta A_i = \sum_{i=1}^{n} F_i \Delta S_i \cos \alpha_i$$

ΔS if we take the limit from (4.4) as it tends to zero

$$A = \lim_{\Delta S \to 0} \left(\sum_{i=1}^{n} F_i \Delta S \right) = \int_S F_\tau dS$$

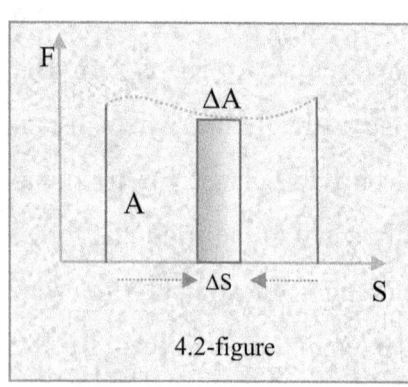

4.2-figure

(4.5) to calculate the integral, it is necessary to know the dependence of the force F□ on the distance S. In practice, it is important not only to know the work performed by the force, but also the time interval in which this work is performed. Therefore, the concept of power is introduced to describe the rate at which work is done by a force. A physical quantity numerically equal to the work done by a force F within a unit of time is called force (N). In other words, the physical quantity that expresses the acceleration of the body's work is called power.

$$N = \frac{\Delta A}{\Delta t}$$

Often, moving machines and mechanisms: airplanes, rockets, satellites, ships, etc. move at a constant speed. Such a movement is equal in magnitude to the resistance force of the moving machines and takes place in the opposite direction. corresponds to, i.e., a=0 and cosa =1, and the work done is A=FS, then the power

$$N = P = \frac{A}{t} = F \cdot \upsilon, \qquad (4.6)$$

Hence, the speed is inversely proportional to the acting force when the power of the moving machine is constant. Based on this principle, the speed distribution of cars works. If the power is variable, we get the limit from (4.6) to determine the power

$$N = \lim_{\Delta t \to 0} \frac{\Delta A}{\Delta t} = \frac{dA}{dt}.$$

This expression is called instantaneous power. Considering (4.3), (4.7a) takes the following form

$$N = F_\tau \frac{dS}{dt} = F_\tau \upsilon.$$

Therefore, the instantaneous power is numerically equal to the tangential component of the force multiplied by the speed when the speed remains constant. When 1 J of work is done for 1 s, the power is equal to 1 W. Horsepower is used to determine the power of cars and other moving mechanisms. 1 o.c. =735 W

Not all of the work done will be useful, some of the work will be wasted (for example, to overcome the frictional force). Therefore, the concept of useful work coefficient (F.I.K.) is introduced. Any moving machine is driven by an engine and designed to do a specific job. During the movement of the engine, the law of conservation of energy is strictly observed, since the amount of energy spent is never greater than the energy received. For example, when the engine of a ground-cultivating tractor is running, one-third of the fuel energy is converted into mechanical energy and does work. The remaining two-thirds of energy is spent on useless work. Futile work is done mainly to overcome the force of resistance. Gainful employment is less than permanent full-time employment. The physical quantity that shows how much or what percentage of the work done is useful is called the coefficient of useful work.

$$\eta = \frac{A_\phi}{A_{yM}} = \frac{N_\phi}{N_{yM}},$$

$$\eta = \frac{A_\phi}{A_{yM}} \cdot 100\% = \frac{N_\phi}{N_{yM}} \cdot 100\%.$$

A_ϕ – the useful part of the work performed (that is, the useful work), Aum - the total work performed (total energy consumed), Nf - the useful power of the device (useful power),

Num - the total power received by the device (total power). It should be remembered that there will always be η<1 or η<100%, because the useful work Af will be a part of the total work Aum. Therefore Af<Aum will be.

Elastic and inelastic impact of balls.

1. Absolute inelastic and elastic shocks.

Collision is a process of short-term interaction of objects in a small area of space. For example, when two steel balls with a diameter of 10 cm collide with each other at a speed of 5 m/s, the interaction lasts only 0.0005 s. But in the process of collision, great forces are finally manifested in the area of contact of the spheres. In particular, in the example mentioned above, the amount of force exerted during the impact exceeds 40,000 N. Objects are deformed during impact. As a result, all or part of the kinetic energy of objects colliding with each other can be converted into potential energy of elastic deformation and internal energy of objects. An increase in internal energy is manifested in an increase in the temperature of bodies. Let's get acquainted with the two limit views of collisions.*a). Absolute inelastic collision.*

Impact of objects consisting of substances such as clay, plasticine, lead. The characteristic features of absolute inelastic impact are as follows:

a) the deformation of the objects formed during the collision is preserved; b) deformation potential energy does not occur;

c) part of the kinetic energy of the bodies is spent on the deformation of the bodies. Due to the preservation of deformation, this part of energy is not restored in the form of kinetic energy, but becomes the internal energy of bodies. Usually this part of the energy is called deformation work;

g) after the collision, the objects move with a common speed or are at relative rest.

Therefore, in an absolutely inelastic collision, only the law of conservation of momentum is fulfilled. The law of conservation of mechanical energy is not fulfilled.

For example, let the spheres m1 and m2 move with velocities $\vec{\vartheta}_1$ and $\vec{\vartheta}_2$ and collide absolutely inelastically. $\vec{\vartheta}_1$ and $\vec{\vartheta}_2$ are directed along the straight line connecting the centers of the spheres. Let's write the law of conservation of momentum for a closed system consisting of two spheres, denoting the speed after the impact by V'

$$m_1\vec{J}_1 + m_2\vec{J}_2 = (m_1 + m_2)\vec{V'}$$

from this

$$\vec{V'} = \frac{m_1\vec{J}_1 + m_2\vec{J}_2}{m_1 + m_2}$$

Based on this expression, we come to the following conclusions

a) if the balls move towards each other (Fig. 4.13a), the direction of joint movement of both balls after impact is |m1ϑ1|

and |m2ϑ2| depends on

b) if the spheres move towards each other, but |m1ϑ1| = |m2ϑ2| if (Fig. 4.13b), after the impact, the balls do not continue their mechanical movements, that is, V' = 0;

c) if the balls move in one direction (Fig. 4.13), even after the collision, they continue to move in that direction. The total kinetic energy the balls have before impact $\frac{m_1 J_1^2}{2} + \frac{m_2 J_2^2}{2}$ and of the total kinetic energy after the collision $\frac{m_1+m_2}{2}*(V')^2$ the difference is equal to the deformation work (Ad).

$$A_D = \frac{m_1 J_1^2}{2} + \frac{m_2 J_2^2}{2} - \frac{m_1 + m_2}{2}*(V')^2$$

If we put its value (4.59) in place of V' and after a series of mathematical operations, we create the following equation

$$A_D = \frac{m_1 + m_2}{2(m_1 + m_2)}*(J_1 + J_2)^2$$

If one of the colliding particles is stationary, the expression (4.61) becomes simpler. For example: if we take $\vartheta_2 = 0$,

$$A_D = \frac{m_1 m_2}{2(m_1 + m_2)}*(J_1)^2 = \frac{m_2}{m_1 + m_2}*\frac{m_1 J_1^2}{2}$$

will be. If the kinetic energy of the first object before impact

$\dfrac{m_1 J_1^2}{2}$ taking into account that (4.62) can be written as follows:

$$A_D = \dfrac{m_2}{m_1 + m_2} * E_1.$$

Therefore, in cases where it is necessary to create larger deformations (for example, in blacksmithing), it is more convenient that the mass of the stationary body (m2)

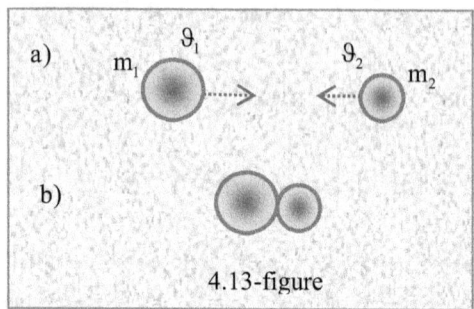

4.13-figure

is greater than the mass of the impacting body (m1). Conversely, when driving a nail or a stake, the mass of the hammer (m1) should be greater than that of the nail or stake.

b). *Absolute elastic impact.*

The impact of objects made of materials such as ivory is very close to an absolutely elastic impact. The characteristic features of absolute elastic impact are as follows:

a) during impact, elastic deformation of objects occurs, but after the impact, it disappears completely, that is, the shape of objects is restored;

b) when objects are deformed, kinetic energy is partially (or completely) transformed into potential energy of elastic deformation, and when objects restore their shape, it is transformed into kinetic energy again, kinetic energy is not transformed into other types of energy, in particular, internal energy;

c) After the collision, the bodies do not move together.

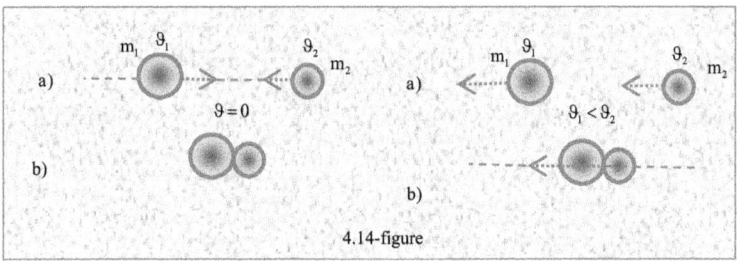

4.14-figure

In absolute elastic impact, the law of conservation of system momentum and the law of conservation of system mechanical energy are fulfilled. These laws are written as follows for the central collision of balls with masses m1 and m2

$$m_1 \vec{J}_1 + m_2 \vec{J}_2 = m_1 \vec{V}_1' + m_2 \vec{V}_2',$$

$$\frac{m_1 J_1^2}{2} + \frac{m_2 J_2^2}{2} = \frac{m_1 (V_1')^2}{2} + \frac{m_2 (V_2')^2}{2}.$$

In these equations, ϑ_1 and ϑ_2 are the velocities of the balls before the collision, and V_1' and V_2' are the velocities after the collision. Solving (4.65) and (4.66) together

$$V_1' = \frac{2m_2 J_2 \pm (m_1 - m_2)J_1}{m_1 + m_2},$$

$$V_2' = \frac{2m_1 J_1 \pm (m_1 - m_2)J_2}{m_1 + m_2}.$$

we create expressions. Let's discuss some special cases.
Let one of the spheres be at rest, i.e. Then the expression (4.67) becomes:

$$V_1' = \frac{m_1 - m_2}{m_1 + m_2} J_1,$$

$$V_2' = \frac{2m_1}{m_1 + m_2} J_1.$$

Therefore, the magnitude of the speed of the balls after the impact depends on the ratio of their masses. If the mass of one of the spheres is finally greater than the other, that is, the condition is fulfilled

$$V_1' = -V_2', \quad V_2' = 0.$$

will be This can happen when an elastic ball hits a wall (the mass and radius of the wall are assumed to be large). Therefore, the value of the speed of the ball hitting the wall is preserved, but its direction changes to the opposite. In other words, the ball bounces back elastically from the wall.
Expressions (4.69) when spheres of equal mass (i.e.) collide

with each other

$V_1' = J_2, \quad V_2' = J_1.$

appears. So, the balls exchange (exchange) their velocities.

EXAMPLES OF PROBLEM SOLVING

Issue 1. A lifting crane has done $2.95 \cdot 10^4$ J of work during the first 5 seconds in the process of lifting a load at rest with an acceleration of 2 m/s2. Determine the mass of the load?

Given: a=2 м/с²; t=5 с; A=29500 Ж; v_0=0.

Need to find: m = ?

Solution: 1. The work done in this case, where the lifting force and the direction of displacement are suitable

$A = F \cdot S$

is equal to

$F - mg = m \cdot a$.

From this

$F = m \cdot (g + a)$

we come to expression.

$S = \dfrac{at^2}{2}$

moves to a distance.

4. Substituting the values of F and S, for the work done:

$$A = F \cdot S = m \cdot (g+a) \cdot \frac{at^2}{2}$$

we form the expression. From this we find the mass of the load.

$$m = \frac{2A}{(g+a)at^2}.$$

5. We calculate:

$$m = \frac{2 \cdot 29500}{\left(9.8\frac{m}{c^2} + 2\frac{m}{c}\right) \cdot 2\frac{m}{c^2} \cdot 25c^2} = 100\,\text{кг}.$$

Answer: m=100 kg.

Issue 2. A bullet weighing 0.08 N is fired from a rifle in a horizontal direction. The target is located at a distance of 400 m, and the bullet drops by 2 m before reaching the target. Find the kinetic energy of the bullet when it leaves the gun.

Given: P=0,08 H, S=400 м, h=2 м.
Need to find: $W_K = ?$
Solution: 1. Kinetic energy of the bullet

$$W_k = \frac{m\upsilon^2}{2}$$

determined using the formula.

2. The bullet is involved in two movements during the flight. Due to the first motion (motion of free fall), the arrow

fell down a distance h. This is for action

$$h = \frac{gt^2}{2}$$

the expression is appropriate. Here we find the time that the bullet should reach the target:

$$t^2 = \frac{2h}{g} \quad \text{ва} \quad t = \sqrt{\frac{2h}{g}}.$$

Due to the second movement (movement in the horizontal direction), the arrow has traveled a distance S in time t. Hence bullet speed

$$v = \frac{S}{t} = \frac{S}{\sqrt{\frac{2h}{g}}} = \sqrt{\frac{g}{2h}} \cdot S$$

should be determined by expression.

3. Putting the speed value in the kinetic energy formula

$$W_K = \frac{mv^2}{2} = \frac{m}{2}\left(S\sqrt{\frac{g}{2h}}\right)^2 = \frac{mgS^2}{4h} = \frac{PS^2}{4h}$$

we form the expression.

4. We calculate:

$$W_K = \frac{0,08H \cdot (400)^2}{4 \cdot 2} = 1600 \text{ Ж}.$$

Answer: The bullet had a kinetic energy of 1600 J when it exited the gun.

Issue 3. A tram moving at a speed of 10 m/s on the

horizontal part of the road was suddenly braked due to an emergency. How far does it slide before it stops? Let the coefficient of friction be 0.2.

Given: $\upsilon=10$ м/с; $\mu=0{,}2$; $g=9{,}8$ м/с².

Need to find: $S=?$

Solution: 1. The change in the kinetic energy of the tram over the distance S is equal to the work done by the frictional force on this road S:

$$\Delta W_K = F_{ишк} \cdot S$$

2. In this case:

$$\Delta W_K = \frac{m\upsilon^2}{2}.$$

Because in the last situation, the speed of the tram (hence the kinetic energy) is zero.

3. This value of ΔW_K and friction force

$$F_{ишк} \cdot S = \mu mg$$

considering that

$$\frac{m\upsilon^2}{2} = \mu \cdot m \cdot g \cdot S$$

we construct the equation From this

$$S = \frac{\upsilon^2}{2 \cdot \mu \cdot g}$$

we form the equation

4. We calculate:

$$S = \frac{\left(10\frac{M}{c}\right)^2}{2 \cdot 0{,}2 \cdot 9{,}8\frac{M}{c^2}} = 25{,}5 \, M.$$

Answer: The tram slides for a distance of 25.5 m.

Issue 4. A ball is thrown vertically down from a height of 10 m with a speed of 14 m/s. How high will the ball rise after hitting the ground?

Given: $h_1 = 10$ м; $\upsilon_1 = 14$ м/с; $g = 9{,}8$ м/с².

Need to find: $h_2 = ?$

Solution: 1. According to the law of conservation of energy, total mechanical energy at height h1 (W1) and total mechanical energy at height h2 is W1=W2.

2. The values of total mechanical energy at height h1 and h2 are determined as follows:

$$W_1 = W_{n_1} + W_{k_1} = mgh_1 + \frac{m\upsilon_1^2}{2},$$

$$W_2 = W_{n_2} + W_{k_2} = mgh_2.$$

3. We equalize the values of W1 and W2

$$mgh_1 + \frac{mv_1^2}{2} = mgh_2.$$

From this

$$h_2 = h_1 + \frac{v_1^2}{2g}.$$

we form the expression.

4. We calculate: $h_2 = 10 \text{м} + \dfrac{\left(14\frac{\text{м}}{\text{с}}\right)^2}{2 \cdot 9{,}8\frac{\text{м}}{\text{с}^2}} = 20 \text{м}.$

Answer: The ball returned from the ground and rose to a height of 20 m.

Issues for independent solution

1. What work must be done to move a body of mass 500 kg with a speed of 10 m/s in 5 s? Assume that the direction of force coincides with the direction of motion. The coefficient of friction is 0.02.

2. A car with a mass of 2·103 started with an acceleration of 20 m/s2 and increased its speed on a horizontal road in 5 s. If the coefficient of resistance is 0.01, how much work will it do at this time?

3. Determine the work done when a body of mass 20 kg is raised from rest to a height of 20 m with uniform acceleration in 10 s. Ignore air resistance.

4. A car with a mass of $3 \cdot 10^3$ kg was raised along the rail up a hill with a slope of 30^0 from the horizon. If it is known that the car is moving with an acceleration of 0.2 m/s^2, what is the work done by the force of gravity on the 50 m track. The coefficient of friction is 0.1.

5. A load of mass 31 kg is moved along a horizontal surface with a constant speed with the help of a force acting at an angle of 60^0 to the horizon. The coefficient of friction is 0.7. 500 J of work was done in raising the body 5 m. What is the magnitude of the force applied to the load?

6. The ends of springs of the same length with stiffnesses of 9.8 and 19.6 N/m are connected in parallel. What work must be done to stretch the springs by 1 cm.

7. If the springs are connected in series, how much work must be done to stretch them (see condition of problem 6).

8. A cube with a side of 6 cm is held under water so that its upper points touch the surface of the water. What is the work done by the pushing force if the cube is released? The density of the cubed substance is 500 kg/m^3.

9. A train with a mass of 10^6 kg traveling on a horizontal track at a speed of 36 km/h stopped after 40 s after braking. Find the average power achieved by the train during braking.

10. A tank with a mass of $3 \cdot 10^4$ kg is climbing a hill with a slope of 30^0 relative to the horizon. If the useful power of the tank is $3.6 \cdot 10^5$ W, what is the maximum speed it can reach?

Ignore resistance to motion.

11. If a car with a mass of 103 kg travels at a constant speed of 36 km/h: a) on a horizontal road; b) to a hill with a slope of 5 m every 100 m; (c) what power will his engine achieve if he descends a hill on the same slope. The coefficient of friction is 0.07.

12. A load with a mass of 10 kg falls freely from a height of 20 m from rest. What is the kinetic energy of the body when it hits the ground, and at what point in its trajectory is the kinetic energy 3 times greater than the potential energy. Ignore air resistance.

CHAPTER V
MECHANICS OF SOLIDS

5.1. Basic concepts about solids

Any body changes its shape and size under the influence of the force applied to it, that is, it is deformed. There is no body in nature that is completely impervious to deformation. But in most cases, bodies are said not to deform when they move. In other words, the distance between two arbitrary points of a rigid

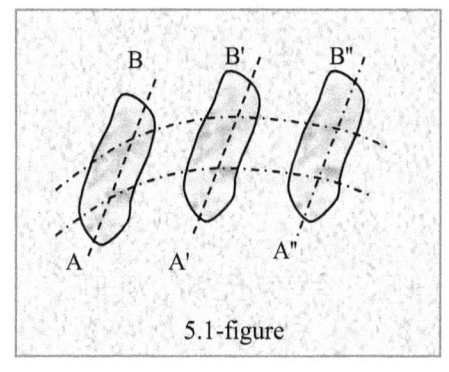

5.1-figure

body is constant. Any motion of a rigid body can be divided into two basic motions: translational motion and rotational motion. In the forward motion of a rigid body, the straight line connecting its two points moves parallel to itself (Fig. 5.1). A solid can be divided into n smaller pieces. But let it be much smaller than the size of each of its pieces. In this case, the solid body can be considered as a system of n material points, and the mass of the solid body m is equal to the sum of these material points:

$$m = \sum_{i=1}^{n} m_i .$$

Here, mi is the mass of particle i. Let us assume that the speed of movement of this piece of solid body is □. A mathematical expression of Newton's second law for such a material point

$$\frac{d}{dt}(m_i v_i) = F_i + f_i$$

will be In this equation, Fi is the internal forces acting on the i-th part of the body, and fi is the equal effector of the external forces acting on this part. If we write the last equation for each part of the solid and take their sum,

$$\sum_{i=1}^{n} \frac{d}{dt}(m_i v_i) = \sum_{i=1}^{n} F_i + \sum_{i=1}^{n} f_i$$

will be Sum of internal forces according to Newton's third law

$$\sum_{i=1}^{n} f_i = 0 \text{ from being}$$

$$\sum_{i=1}^{n} \frac{d}{dt}(m_i v_i) = \sum_{i=1}^{n} F_i$$

or

$$\frac{d}{dt} \sum_{i=1}^{n}(m_i v_i) = \sum_{i=1}^{n} F_i = F.$$

If a rigid body moves only forward, the acceleration of all its points will be the same. Therefore,

$$\frac{d}{dt}\left(\sum_{i=1}^{n} m_i v_i\right) = \sum_{i=1}^{n} m_i \cdot \frac{dv}{dt}$$

we write in the form and $\sum_{i=1}^{n} m_i = m$ taking into account that, we can write it in the following form

$$m \frac{dv}{dt} = F$$

This equation is the forward motion equation of a rigid body and

$$\sum_{i=1}^{n} F_i = F$$

and the equation is referred to as the principal vector of external forces acting on the body or the equal effector of external forces. Comparing these equations with the equation of motion of a material point, we come to the following idea: the forward movement of a solid body can be considered as a material point equal to the mass of the observed solid body is moving under the influence of the main vector of external forces. If the motion of a rigid body is complex, then such motion cannot be replaced by the motion of a single material point, since each point of it has its own acceleration.

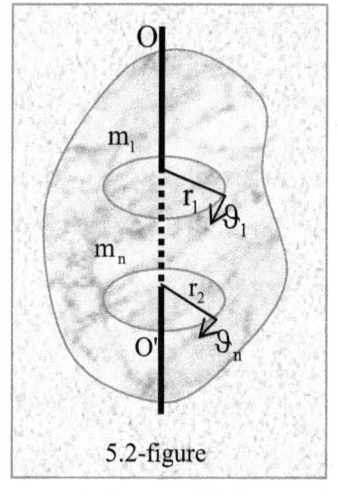

5.2-figure

$m\dfrac{dv}{dt}=F$ The equation is appropriate for the motion of the center of mass of the mechanical system $\dfrac{d(mv_s)}{dt}=F$ comparing with the equation, we are sure that this point, whose motion is equivalent to the motion of a rigid body of mass m, is the center of mass of the rigid body. Therefore, the center of mass of a body acts like a material point such that the mass of this point is equal to the mass of the rigid body and is acted upon by an equal external force..

5.2. Moment of inertia and kinetic energy of a rigid body rotating about a fixed axis.

Let's consider an absolute rigid body rotating around the fixed OO' axis (Fig. 5.2). Let the solid body under investigation consist of n material points. Let the masses of material points be m1, m2 ,..., mn, external forces acting on them F1, F2 , ..., Fn, linear velocities ϑ1, ϑ2 , ..., ϑn and angular velocity ω. To find the rotational kinetic energy of an object, we find the kinetic energy of each material point and then sum them

$$\dfrac{m_1\vartheta_1^2}{2}=\dfrac{m_1}{2}(\omega\cdot r_1)^2 = m_1 r_1^2 \dfrac{\omega^2}{2},$$

$$\dfrac{m_2\vartheta_2^2}{2}=\dfrac{m_2}{2}(\omega\cdot r_2)^2 = m_2 r_2^2 \dfrac{\omega^2}{2},$$

....

$$\dfrac{m_n\vartheta_n^2}{2}=\dfrac{m_n}{2}(\omega\cdot r_n)^2 = m_n r_n^2 \dfrac{\omega^2}{2},$$

or

$$\sum_{i=1}^{n}\frac{m_i\vartheta_i^2}{2}=\sum_{i=1}^{n}m_i r_i^2\frac{\omega^2}{2}.$$

(5.1) – in equality

$$\sum_i \frac{m_i\vartheta_i^2}{2}=Z$$

and

$$\sum_i m_i r_i^2 = J$$

we write the expression of the kinetic energy of a rigid body rotating around a fixed axis as

$$Z=\frac{J\omega^2}{2}.$$

This is the kinetic energy of a body in forward motion ($E_k = \frac{m\vartheta^2}{2}$) comparing with , it follows that the moment of inertia of a body in rotational motion J is a measure of the body's inertia. The greater the moment of inertia of the body, the more energy must be expended for the body to gain a greater speed. (5.2) is called the moment of inertia of the body J in relation to the axis of rotation OO'. (5.2) - it follows from the equation that the moment of inertia of a material point is equal to the mass of the material point multiplied by the square of the distance from the point to the axis of rotation

$$J = mr^2.$$

According to the equation (5.4), the moment of inertia of the body in the international system of units is measured in kg·m2. The energy of a wheeled body moving on a horizontal plane is the sum of its kinetic energy in forward motion and rotational motion of the body.

$$W = \frac{m\vartheta^2}{2} + \frac{J\omega^2}{2}.$$

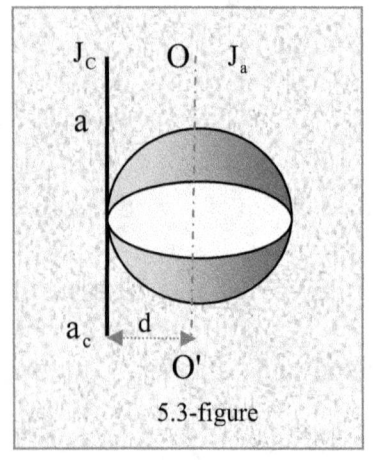

5.3-figure

Strictly speaking, the mass m of the body should be considered as a continuously distributed mechanical system over its volume V, in which the moment of inertia of the body

$$J = \int_{(m)} \rho^2 dm = \int_{(V)} \rho^2 D dV$$

will be Here, D is the density of the body, and is the mass of a small element of volume dV at a distance □ from the axis of rotation of the body. The moment of inertia of an object depends on its material, shape, size, as well as its location relative to the axis of rotation of the object.

If Steiner's theorem is used, it becomes easier to calculate the moment of inertia of an object about an arbitrary axis: the moment of inertia of an object about an arbitrary axis a, parallel to this axis, and the moment of inertia of an object about an axis passing through the center of mass S is equal to the sum of Js and the product of the mass m of the object by the square of the distance between these axes (Figure 5.3)

$$J_a = J_C + md^2$$

We prove this theorem. In Figure 5.3, the axes a and as are directed perpendicular to the drawing plane, and the distances from the small element of the body with mass dm to these axes are marked by a and as. Theorem of cosines

$$\rho^2 = \rho_0^2 + d^2 + d\rho_c \cos\varphi$$

according to

$$J_a = \int_{(m)} \rho^2 dm = \int_{(m)} \rho_c^2 dm + md^2 + 2d \int_{(m)} x^* dm$$

will be. Here $x^* = \rho_c \cdot \cos\varphi$ - the origin of the element dm of the body is at the center of mass of the body, and its abscissa is the abscissa in the coordinate system intersecting with the a and as axes and perpendicular to the plane on which they lie. From the definition (5.4) of the center of mass

$$\int_{(m)} x^* dm = mx_c^* = 0$$

because the center of mass of the object coincides with the coordinate origin. Thus, the correctness of relation (5.7) was proved. Let's see some examples of calculating moments of inertia of simple bodies.

Example 1. We find the moment of inertia about the axis of a thin-walled circular cylinder of mass m and radius R. All small elements of such a cylinder are located at the same distance R from the axis passing through its center of mass S. Therefore

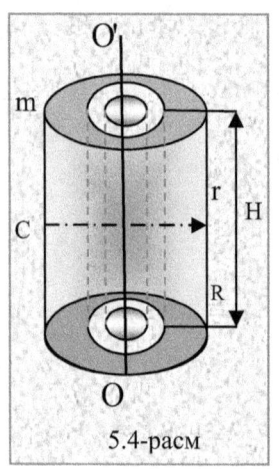

5.4-расм

will be.

Example 2. We find the moment of inertia about the axis of a homogeneous solid cylinder of mass m and radius R. We divide the cylinder into a large number of thin cylinders with a common axis. Suppose the radius of one of them is r, and the thickness of its wall is dr<<r. This is the moment of inertia of the small cylinder element

$$dJ_C = r^2 \, dm = 2\pi r^2 \, rHD \, dr$$

will be Here N is the height of the cylinder; D is its density. We find the moment of inertia of a complete cylinder by summing up the moments of inertia of all its small elements, i.e. by integrating the expression (5.9) from 0 to

$$RJ_C = 2\pi HD \int_0^R r^2 dr = \frac{1}{2}\pi R^2 HD = \frac{mR^2}{2}$$

here $m = \pi DR^2 H$ the mass of the cylinder (Fig. 5.4).

Example 3. We find the moment of inertia of a homogeneous thin rod of mass m and length l about an axis passing through its center. We divide the sturgeon into small pieces. Let's say that x is the distance of one such piece to the axis of rotation, and dx is the length of the piece. Then this is the moment of inertia of the element

$$dJ_c = x^2 dm = x^2 DS dx$$

Will be. Here S is the cross-sectional surface of the stern; D- its density. We find the moment of inertia of the first half of the boom by integrating the expression (5.11) over x from 0 to l/2, the moment of inertia of the entire boom is twice as large

$$J_c = 2DS \int_0^{1/2} x^2 dx = \frac{2}{3}DS\left(\frac{1}{2}\right)^3 = \frac{ml^2}{12},$$

because the mass of the stern is . And finally, we present the moment of inertia of a homogeneous sphere of mass m and radius R about an axis passing through its center

5.3. Moment of force. Angular momentum and its law of change. The fundamental equation of the dynamics of rotational motion

Suppose a solid consists of n material points. Material point masses m1, m2 ,..., mn , acting external forces F1, F2 , ... Fn, distances from the axis of rotation to the solid body r1, r2, ... rn, linear velocities ϑ_1, ϑ_2, ..., ϑ_n and let us denote the angular velocity by ω. We find the forces acting on material points according to the second law of dynamics, and then we get their sum

$$F_1 = m_1 \frac{d\vartheta_1}{dt} = m_1 r_1 \cdot \frac{d\omega}{dt} = m_1 r_1 \varepsilon,$$

$$F_2 = m_2 \frac{d\vartheta_2}{dt} = m_2 r_2 \cdot \frac{d\omega}{dt} = m_2 r_2 \varepsilon,$$

....

$$F_n = m_n \frac{d\vartheta_n}{dt} = m_n r_n \cdot \frac{d\omega}{dt} = m_n r_n \varepsilon.$$

(5.14) - multiply both sides of the system of equations by: and add

$$F_1 r_1 + F_2 r_2 + ... + F_n r_n = (m_1 r_1^2 + m_2 r_2^2 + ... m_n r_n^2)\varepsilon$$

or

$$M_1 + M_2 + ... + M_n = (J_1 + J_2 + ... J_n)\varepsilon$$

In that case

$$M_1 + M_2 + ... + M_n = M$$

and

$$J_1 + J_2 + ... J_n = J$$

if we define as (5.15)-equation

$$M = J \cdot \varepsilon$$

we write in the form. (5.16) - equality expresses the second law of dynamics for circular motion. According to this equation, the moment of rotational force exerted on a body is equal to the product of the body's moment of inertia times its angular acceleration. It can be seen from the equation (5.16) that the angular acceleration ($\square$) generated by the turning moment changes depending on the moment of inertia of the body, that is, the greater the moment of inertia of the body, the smaller the angular acceleration. The moment of the force F with respect to the stationary point O is defined as the vector product of this force with the radius-vector r transferred from the point O to the point N where the force F is applied.

$$\vec{M} = \left[\vec{r} \cdot \vec{F} \right].$$

The vector M is directed perpendicular to the plane of vectors r and F according to the right drill rule (Fig. 5.5). Modulus of torque

M=F·r sinα=F·ℓ

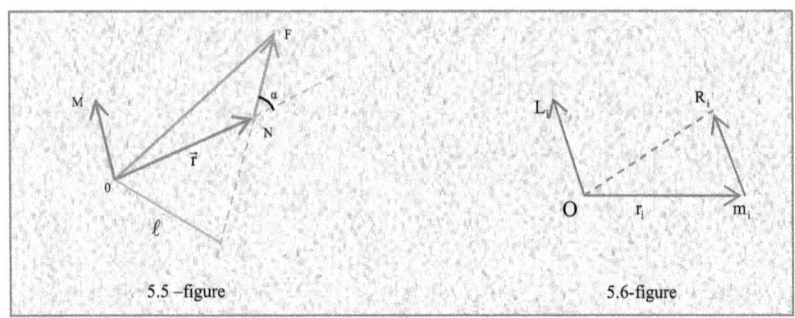

5.5–figure   5.6-figure

determined by the formula. Here $\square$ is the angle between r and F, - the length of the vertical line drawn from point 0 to the line of action of force F. In this case, the quantity F is called the shoulder of the force.

5.4. Impulse moment

point O (Fig. 5.6)

$$\vec{L}_i = \left[\vec{r}_i m_i \vec{V}_i\right] = \left[\vec{r}_i \vec{P}_i\right].$$

Accordingly, the moment of impulse of a mechanical system relative to a fixed point O is a vector equal to the geometric sum of the impulse moments of all material points of the system relative to this point

We get the expression (5.20) differentially with respect to time t

$$\frac{d\vec{L}}{dt} = \frac{d}{dt}\sum_{i=1}^{n}[\vec{r}_i\vec{P}_i] = \sum_{i=1}^{n}\frac{d}{dt}[\vec{r}_i\vec{P}_i] = \sum_{i=1}^{n}[\vec{r}_i\frac{d\vec{p}_i}{dt}]$$

because

$$\left[\frac{d\vec{r}_i}{dt}\right] = [\vec{V}_i\vec{P}_i] = 0.$$

From expressions (5.19) and (5.20).

$$\frac{d\vec{L}}{dt} = \frac{d}{dt}\sum_{i=1}^{n}[\vec{r}_i\vec{F}_i^{\,òàø}] + \sum_{i=1}^{n}\left[\vec{r}_i\sum_{k=1}^{n}\vec{F}_{ik}\right]$$

it turns out to be. The vector equal to the geometric sum of moments of all external forces acting on the mechanical system relative to point O is called the main moment of external forces relative to point O.

EXAMPLES OF PROBLEM SOLVING

Issue 1. 0072=a load M=500 g is hung on the end of a string wound on a coil with a radius of 15 cm. If the load is falling down with an acceleration of a=100 cm/s2, find the moment of inertia of the coil.

Given: M= 500 г=0,5 kg; r =15 sm = 0,15 m; a=100 sm/s²=1m/s².

Need to find: I= ?

Solution: The basic equation of motion of a rigid body is:

$M = I \cdot \varepsilon$,

where M is the turning moment, ☐ is the angular acceleration, and I is the moment of inertia. The torque M causes the string tension force T, so:

$M = r \cdot T$.

To find the tension force of the string, we apply Newton's second law to the load, i.e $F = m \cdot a$, бунда $m = \dfrac{P}{g}$,

$F = P - T$ from the fact that:

$\dfrac{P}{g} \cdot a = P - T$

From that

$T = P\left(1 - \dfrac{a}{g}\right)$.

Substituting (3) into (2):

$M = P \cdot r \left(1 - \dfrac{\alpha}{g}\right)$,

where P =mg is the weight of the load. According to the

condition of the matter $\varepsilon = \dfrac{a}{r}$, because the linear speed of the spool flange points is equal to the speed of the load

$$I = \dfrac{M}{\varepsilon} = \dfrac{M \cdot r}{a} = \dfrac{P \cdot r^2}{a}\left(1 - \dfrac{a}{g}\right)$$

or since P=mg, we write (5) in the following form:

$$I = \dfrac{mr^2}{a}(g-a).$$

We calculate:

$$I = \dfrac{0{,}5\,\text{кг} \cdot (0{,}15\,\text{m}^2)}{0{,}96\,\dfrac{\text{m}}{\text{с}^2}} \cdot \left(9{,}8\,\dfrac{\text{m}}{\text{с}^2} - 1\,\dfrac{\text{m}}{\text{с}^2}\right) \approx 0{,}0979\,\text{кг}\cdot\text{m}^2.$$

Answer: I=0,0979 kg·m².

Issue 2. If a 10 kBt motor rotates 3000 times in 1 minute, find its torque.

Given: N=10 кВт=10^4 Вт, n=3000 айл/мин=50 айл/с.
Need to find: M=?
Solution: Formula of power:

$$N = \frac{dA}{dt} = \frac{Md\varphi}{dt} = M\omega.$$

Angular speed of the motor: $\omega = 2\pi n = 2 \cdot 3{,}14 \cdot 50 = 314\frac{1}{s}.$

motor torque:

$$M = \frac{N}{\omega}$$

is found from the formula. We calculate:

$$M = \frac{N}{\omega} = \frac{10^4 \text{Вт}}{314\frac{1}{s}} \approx 31{,}84 \text{Н} \cdot \text{м}$$

Answer: M=31,84 Н·м.

Issue 3. A disk-shaped block of mass m = 0.06 kg is passed through a thin string. Loads m1=0.2kg and m2=0.3kg are hung from the ends of the string. If these loads are left free, with what acceleration will they move? Ignore friction.

Given: m=0,06 кг, m_1=0,2 кг, m_2=0,3 кг.

Need to find: a=?

Solution: Method 1 We use the basic laws of forward and circular motions to solve the problem. Each moving load is affected by two forces: the downward tension force P=mg and the upward thread tension force T (Fig.1a).

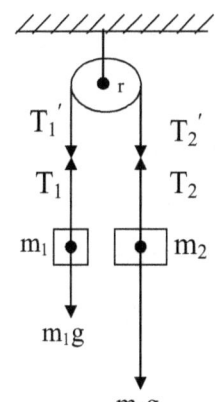 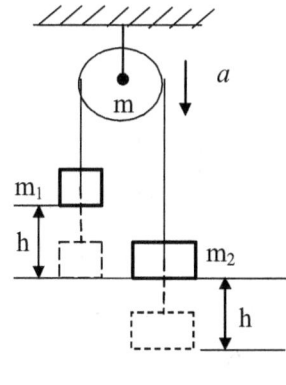

The load m1 moves up, so T1>m1g. According to Newton's second law, the equal effector of these forces is equal to their difference, and is directly proportional to the mass of the load and its acceleration.

$T_1 - m_1 \cdot g = m_1 a$,

From this

$T_1 = m_1 g + m_1 a$.

The load m2 is downward, so T2 < m2g. We write the second law formula for this load:

$m_2 g - T_2 = m_2 a$,

From this

$T_2 = m_2 g - m_2 a$.

$M = I \cdot \varepsilon$.

forces T1 and T2, respectively, but opposite in direction. As the loads move, the disc rotates clockwise, so $T'_2 > T'_1$. The torque exerted on the disc is equal to the product of the difference of these forces by the radius of the disc, i.e.

$M = (T'_2 - T'_1) r$.

Moment of inertia of the disc

$I = \dfrac{mr^2}{2}$.

Angular acceleration with linear acceleration of loads $\varepsilon = \dfrac{a}{r}$ linked by relationship. Putting the expressions M, I in the formula (3), we find the following:

$(T'_2 - T'_1) \cdot r = \dfrac{mr^2}{2} \cdot \dfrac{a}{r}$,

From this

$T'_2 - T'_1 = \dfrac{m}{2} \cdot a$.

$T'_1 = T_1$ ва $T'_2 = T_2$ for being T'_1 ва T'_2 forces can be replaced by expressions in the formula (1) and (2), then:

$m_2 g - m_2 a - m_1 g - m_1 a = \dfrac{m}{2} a$

or

$$(m_2 - m_1)g = \left(m_2 - m_1 + \frac{m}{2}\right)a,$$

From this

$$a = \frac{m_2 - m_1}{m_2 - m_1 + \frac{m}{2}} g.$$

We calculate:

$$a = \frac{0,3 \text{ кг} - 0,2 \text{ кг}}{0,3 \text{ кг} + 0,2 \text{ кг} + \frac{0,06 \text{ кг}}{2}} \cdot 9,81 \frac{\text{м}}{\text{с}^2} = 1,85 \frac{\text{м}}{\text{с}^2}.$$

Answer: $a = 1,85$ m/s^2.

Method 2. In solving the problem, we use the law of conservation of energy, according to this law, the total energy of a system of isolated bodies in the absence of friction remains unchanged during the movement of these bodies. In this case, energy can only be transferred from potential energy to kinetic energy or vice versa. Let us remind you that in mechanics, the total energy of a body is the sum of its potential and kinetic energies. Let the potential energy of the first load be equal to P1 and that of the second to P2 at the beginning of the movement. After some time, the height of the first load increased by h, and that of the second decreased by h (Fig. 1). The potential energy of the first charge is P1+m1□gh, and the second one is P2 - m2gh. In addition, each of the loads moves with acceleration □, during this time □ according to the speed $\frac{m_1\upsilon^2}{2}$ билан $\frac{m_2\upsilon^2}{2}$ achieves a kinetic energy equal to Similarly, the disk is moving uniformly with an angular velocity □ and is related to it $\frac{I\omega^2}{2}$ gains kinetic energy. We change the expression for the kinetic energy of the disc and write:

$$I = \frac{mr^2}{2} \quad \text{ва} \quad \omega = \frac{\upsilon}{r}$$

for being

$$\frac{1}{2}I\omega^2 = \frac{1}{2}\frac{mr^2}{2} \cdot \frac{\upsilon^2}{r^2} = \frac{mr^2}{4}.$$

According to the law of conservation of energy:

$$Ï_1 + Ï_2 = Ï_1 + m_1gh + Ï_2 - m_2gh + \frac{m_1\upsilon^2}{2} + \frac{m_2\upsilon^2}{2} + \frac{m\upsilon^2}{2}.$$

(6)

We move the terms related to the potential energy of loads

from the right part of (6) to the left part. After certain modifications, the following is generated:

$$(m_2-m_1)gh = \left(m_2-m_1+\frac{m}{2}\right)\frac{v^2}{2}.$$

Since the loads move with uniform acceleration $v^2 = 2ah$.

So, $(m_2-m_1)g = \left(m_2+m_1+\frac{m}{2}\right)a$,

From this

$$a = \frac{m_2-m_1}{m_2+m_1+\frac{m}{2}} \cdot g,$$

that is, the result corresponding to the expression (5) is obtained.

speed of 5 km/h relative to the stage, how many times per minute will the stage begin to rotate? Consider the stage as a homogeneous circular disk, and the actors as material points. Neglect frictional forces.

Given: r = 12 м; M = 1,2 T=1200 kg; t = (60+70) kg=130 kg; R = 6 m;

v=5 km/hour=1,39 m/s.

Need to find: v =?

Solution: When the stage and the performers are at rest, their angular momentum is zero. When the artists start walking, the stage also moves, and their collective moments of momentum

$I_1\omega_1 = I_2\omega_2$

is, based on the law of conservation of angular momentum:

$I_1\omega_1 + I_2\omega_2 = 0$,

in this $I_1 = mr^2$ - moments of inertia of artists, ω_1 - their angular velocity, $I_2 = \frac{1}{2}mR^2 + mr^2$ - moment of inertia of the scene together with the artists, P - stage radius, k - the radius of the artists' trajectory, ω_2 - the angular velocity of the scene, $m = m_1 + m_2 = 130$ kg – the total mass of artists. Putting these into the law of conservation of angular momentum, we calculate how many times the scene rotates per minute

$$mr^2 \cdot \frac{\upsilon}{r} + \left(\frac{1}{2}MR^2 + mr^2\right)\omega_2 = 0,$$

From this

$$\omega_2 = -\frac{mr^2 \frac{\upsilon}{r}}{\frac{1}{2}MR^2 + mr^2} = -\frac{2m\upsilon r}{MR^2 + 2mr^2}.$$

But $\omega_2 = 2\pi\nu$ Since the rotation frequency of the stage is:

$$v = \frac{\omega_2}{2\pi} = -\frac{2m\upsilon r}{2\pi(MR^2 + 2mr^2)} = -\frac{130\text{кг} \cdot 1{,}39\frac{\text{м}}{\text{с}} \cdot 6\text{м}}{3{,}14(1200\text{кг} \cdot 12^2\text{м}^2 + 2 \cdot 130\text{кг} \cdot 36\text{м}^2)} =$$

$$= -\frac{1084{,}2}{547952} = -0{,}002\text{с}^{-1} = -0{,}12\frac{\text{айл}}{\text{мин}}.$$

Answer: v=0,12 rot/min

Issues for independent solution

1. The front of the car sinks when braking sharply. Why?
2. 8 cm was cut from one end of the iron rod and 16 cm from the other end. Where and by how much has the center of gravity of the rest of the stern moved.
3. A pipe with weight R=1.2 □104 N is lying on the ground. What force is required to lift it with a crane from one end?
4. A rod of length 1 m and mass 5 kg is suspended horizontally on two parallel strings of the same length. A load of mass 10 kg is attached to the stem at a distance of 0.25 m from one end. Determine the tension of the strings.

Used literature

"A perfect generation - the foundation of Uzbekistan's development" Tashkent-1997.

"National personnel training program". Tashkent-1997.

State educational standard and curriculum of general secondary education. "Sharq" publishing house-printing concern-1999. 4th special issue.

M. Olmasova, J. Kamolov, T. Lutfullaev. Physics (mechanics, molecular physics and heat) T. "Teacher", 1987.

V.G. Razumovsky, B.M. Mirzakhmedov and others. "Fundamentals of physics teaching methodology" T. "Teacher", 1990.

M. Ismoilov, P. Khabibullaev, M. Khalilulin. "Physics course" Tashkent-2000.

M. Rakhmatullaev. "General physics course" (Mechanics) T. "Teacher", 1995.

V.A. Balash "Problems of physics", T. "Teacher", 1966.

V. M. Spiransky. How to solve physics problems. -T.: Teacher. 1971.

С.Е.Каманецкий, В.П.Орехов «Физикадан масалалар ечиш методикаси», Т. Ўқитувчи, 1976 й.

M. Ismailov. A set of problems from physics. - T.: Teacher. 1966.

K.A. Tursunmetov and others. "Collection of problems from physics", T. "Teacher", 2001.

M.E. Tulchinsky "Sbornik kachestvennyx zadach po fizike", M., Prosveshchenie, 1965.

S.S. Moshkov. Experimental physics. - M.: 1955.

L. I. Reznikov "Graphic method and physics teaching" M. 1960

V. G. Razumovsky "Tvorcheskie zadachi po fizike v sredney shkol" M., Prosveshchenie, 1966.

O. I. Ahmadjanov. Physics course part 1, Tashkent, "Teacher" 1989

A.S. Safarov. General physics course, Tashkent, "Teacher". 1992

S.P. Strelkov Mechanics, Tashkent, "Teacher", 1977.

V.S. Volkenstein. A set of problems from the General Physics course. Tashkent, "Teacher". 1979.

V. I. Iveronova. Physics practicum, Tashkent, "Teacher", 1971.

R.I. Grabovsky. General physics, Tashkent, "Teacher", 1974

N.A. Sultanov Physics course, Fergana, "Technika", 2002.

E.N. Nazirov, Z.A. Khudoyberganov, N.Kh. Safiullina Practical training in mechanics and molecular physics, Tashkent, "Teacher", 2001.

T. Turgunov Practical physics, "Uzbekistan", 2003.

M. Sh. Haydarova, U. K. Nazarov laboratory works in physics. "Teacher" 1989.

S. A. Budarina, A. A. Israelov. Laboratory exercises in physics. "Teacher" 1993.

B Yavorsky, A. Detlaf. Physics, "Drofa", Moscow 2003.

M. Mominov, Kh. Haydarov. Handbook for laboratory work in physics. "Teacher" – 1971

M. Ismoilov, P. Habibbullaev, M. Khaliulin Physics course, "Teacher", 2000

APPLICATIONS

The main international system of units

Quantities		Quantities	
Name	**Size**	**Name**	**Designation**
Length	Л	Meter	M
Mass	M	Kilogram	Кг
Time	T	In a second	С
Current strength	И	Ampere	A
Thermod.temp.	Θ	Kelvin	К
Amount of substance	ν	rich	Мол
Light power	Ж	candela	кд

Derivative units

Name	Size	Designation
Surface	L^2	m^2
Volume	L^3	m^3
Speed	LT^{-1}	m/s
Acceleration	LT^{-2}	m/s^2
Frequency	T^{-1}	Gs
Angular velocity	T^{-1}	rad/s
Angular acceleration	T^{-2}	rad/s^2
Density	$L^{-3}M$	kg/m^3

Quantity	Dimension	Unit
Moment of inertia	L^2M	$kg \cdot m^2$
Impulse's	LMT^{-1}	$kg \cdot m/s^2$
Moment of impulse	L^2MT^{-1}	$kg \cdot m^2/s$
Strength	LMT^{-2}	H
Moment of force	L^2MT^{-2}	$N \cdot m$
Power impulse	LMT^{-1}	$N \cdot s$
Pressure	$L^{-1}MT^{-2}$	Ra
Work, energy	L^2MT^{-2}	DJ
Power	L^2MT^{-3}	WT
Dynamic viscosity	$L^{-1}MT^{-1}$	$Pa \cdot s$
Kinematic viscosity Heat content	L^2T^{-1}	$м^2/с$
Comparative iss. quantity	L^2MT^{-2}	J
	L^2T^{-2}	J/kg

Some astronomical magnitudes

Name of astronomical magnitude	Numeric value
Mean radius of the Earth	$6.37 \cdot 10^6$ m
Average density of land	$5.5 \cdot 10^3$ kg/m3
Earth's mass	$5{,}96 \cdot 10^{24}$ kg
The radius of the sun	$6{,}95 \cdot 10^8$ m
Average density of the Sun	$1.4 \cdot 10^3$ kg/m^3
The mass of the sun	$1{,}97 \cdot 10^{30}$ kg

The radius of the moon	$1{,}74 \cdot 10^6$ m
The mass of the moon	$7{,}3 \cdot 10^{22}$ kg
The distance to the centers of the Earth and the Moon	$3{,}84 \cdot 10^8$ m
The distance to the centers of the Earth and the Sun	$1{,}5 \cdot 10^{11}$ m
The period of rotation of the moon around the earth	27 days 7 hours 43 minutes

3. Transition from the value of physical quantities expressed in one unit to the value expressed in another unit.

First unit	The second unit	The relationship between the two units
rotation (rot)	degrees (---0)	1 rot = 360^0
rotation (rot)	minute (---)	1 rot = 21600'
rotation (rot)	radian (rad)	1 rot = 6,28 рад
rotation (rot)	second	1 rot = 1296000''
ampere distribution meter (A/m)	ersted	1(А/м)=$12{,}56 \cdot 10^{-3}$ э
watt (W)	horse power (hp)	1 W = $1{,}3596 \cdot 10^{-3}$ о.к.
watt (W)	calorie distribution sec (cal/s)	1 W =0,23884 kal/c
weber (Vb)	Maxwell (Mks)	1 W = $1 \cdot 10^8$ Мкс

gauss (Gs)	tesla (Tl)	1 Gs = 1·10⁻⁴ Тл
henry (Gn)	centimeter (cm)	1 Gn = 1·10⁹ sm
degrees (...⁰)	radian (rad)	1⁰=1,7453·10⁻² rad
degrees (...⁰)	rotation (rot)	1⁰ = 2,77.10⁻³ rot
degrees (...⁰)	minute (...')	1⁰ = 60'
degrees (...⁰)	second (...'')	1⁰ = 3600''
Dina (din).	newton (N)	1 дин = 1·10⁻⁵ Н
joule (J)	erg	1 Ж = 1·10⁷ erg
joule (J)	kilowatt-hour (kWh)	1Ж=2,7777.10⁷ kWh
joule (J)	calories (cal)	1Ж = 0,23889 kal
joule (J)	electron-volt (eV)	1Ж= 6,2418.10¹⁸ eV
Year	week	1йил=52,178 week
Year	a day	1йил=3,6524·10² day
Year	hour	1year = 8,7657.10³ H
Year	minute (min)	1year=5,25·10⁵ min
Year	second (s)	1year= 3,1556.10⁷ c
calories (cal)	joule (J)	1 cal = 4,1868 J
calories (cal)	kilowatt-hour (kWh)	1 cal =1,1627.10⁶ kWh
kelvin (K)	degree celsius (0C)	1 K = 1 ⁰C
kilowatt-hour (kWh)	Joule (J)	1 kWh =3,6·10⁶ J
kilowatt-hour	calories (cal)	1kWh=

(kWh)		$8,6001 \cdot 10^5$ кал
kilogram (kg)	tons (t)	$1 \text{ kg}=1 \cdot 10^{-3}\text{t}$
kilogram (kg)	quintal (s)	$1 \text{ kg}=1 \cdot 10^{-2}\text{s}$
kilogram (kg)	atomic unit of mass	$1\text{kg}=6,022 \cdot 10^{26}\text{mab}$
mileage distribution hour (km/h)	meter distribution second (m/s)	1 km/h =0,27778 m/s
liter (l)	cubic centimeter (cm3)	$1l=1 \cdot 10^3 \text{sm}^3$
liter (l)	cubic meter (m3)	$1l=1 \cdot 10^{-3} \text{м}^3$
Maxwell (Mks)	weber (Vb)	$1 \text{ Mks} =1 \cdot 10^{-8} \text{ Vb}$
atomic unit of mass (b.c.)	kilogram (kg)	$1\text{mab}=1,6505 \cdot 10^{-27}\text{kg}$
megaelectronvolt (MeV)	Joule	$1 \text{ MeV} =1,60218 \cdot 10^{-19} \text{ J}$
meter to second (m/s)	mileage hour (km/h)	1 m/s =3,6 km/h
millimeter of mercury (mm.sim.ust.)	pascal (Pa)	$1\text{mm.sim.ust.}= =1,33322 \cdot 10^2 \text{Pa}$
minute (min)	second (s)	1 min=60 sek
minute (min)	Hour	$1\text{min}=1,666 \cdot 10^{-2}$ hour
minute (min)	radian (rad)	$1'= 2,9088 \cdot 10^{-4} \text{ rad}$
minute (min)	rotation (rot)	$1' =4,633 \cdot 10^{-5} \text{ rot}$
minute (min)	degree (...")	$1'=0,01666^0$
minute (min)	second (...")	$1'=60''$

newton (N)	Dina (din).	$1H = 1 \cdot 10^5 din$
ohm-meter (Ohm m)	om-millimeter square distribution meter (Om.mm2)/m	$1 \text{ Ohm m} = 1 \cdot 10^6 \dfrac{Om \cdot mm^2}{m}$
horse power (hp)	watt (W)	$1hp = 7,35498 \cdot 10^2$ w;
pascal (Pa)	Physical atmosphere (atm)	$1Pa = 9,662 \cdot 10^6 atm$
pascal (Pa)	technical atmosphere (at)	$1Pa = 1,0196 \cdot 10^{-5} at$
pascal (Pa)	millimeter of mercury (mm.sim.ust)	$1Па = 7,5 \cdot 10^{-5}$ mm.sim.ust
radian (rad)	rotation (rot)	1 rad = 0,159 rot
radian (rad)	degree (...^{0})	1 rad = $57,296^0$
radian (rad)	minute (...')	1 rad = 3438'
radian (rad)	second (...")	1 rad = 206300"
секунд (с)	minute (min)	$1 c = 1,666 \cdot 10^{-2} min$
second (s)	Hour	$1 c = 2,776 \cdot 10^{-4} hour$
second (s)	radian (rad)	$1'' = 4,8481 \cdot 10^{-6} rad$
second (s)	rotation (rot)	$1'' = 7,716 \cdot 10^{-7} rot$
second (s)	degree (...^{0})	$1'' = (2,277 \cdot 10^{-4})^0$
second (s)	minute (...')	$1'' = (1,6666 \cdot 10^{-2})'$
Technical atmosphere (at)	pascal (Pa)	$1at = 9,8066 \cdot 10^4 Pa$
Technical atmosphere (at)	physical atmosphere	1 at = 0,96784 atm

Technical atmosphere (at)	millimeters of mercury above. (mm.sim.ust)	1ат=735, mm.sim.ust
Tons (t)	kilogram (kg)	1т=1·10³kg
Physical atmosphere (atm)	pascal (Pa)	1атм=1,0133·10⁵Pa
degree celsius (0S)	Kelvin (K)	1⁰C=1K
electron volt (eV)	Joule (J)	1eV=1,60218.10⁻¹⁹J
Erg	Joule (J)	1 erg=1·10⁻⁷J
ersted (E)	ampere distribution meter (A/m)	1e=79,5775A/m

www.ingramcontent.com/pod-product-compliance
Lightning Source LLC
LaVergne TN
LVHW020439070526
838199LV00063B/4790